Custom Painting
Cars ■ Trucks ■ Motorcycles

JoAnn Bortles

motorbooks

First published in 2008 by MBI Publishing Company and Motorbooks, an imprint of MBI Publishing Company, 400 First Avenue North, Suite 300, Minneapolis, MN 55401 USA

About the Author:

JoAnn Bortles is a nationally recognized and award winning custom painter. Her work has been featured in dozens of magazines and she has written four books on custom painting techniques for Motorbooks, including the bestselling *How to Master Airbrush Painting Techniques*. She lives and works in Waxhaw, North Carolina, running her own custom painting shop, Crazy Horse Painting.

Contents

Acknowledgments

Thanks to the incredible Bill Streeter for all the photos and his amazing artwork.

Thanks to Ron Gibbs, the Canadian Rat Fink, who provided many wonderful photos of his work, and to Aaron Stevenson who also provided studio photos of my paint work.

Many thanks to Dan-Am SATA USA. Their spray equipment makes my life easier and they are wonderful people.

Thanks also to the following: Bent and Knut Jorgenson; Tony Larimer; Scott Barlow of Belaire Compressors; Gary Glass and Iwata Medea; Keith Ball; Darren Williams of Liquid Illusions; Dave Perewitz; Keith Hanson; Mike Jacobs; Ben Jordan; Bill Steele; Jon Kosmoski; Peter Schletty; Darwin Holmstrom; Ron Anderson; Skip Chance and John Hall of House of Kolor; Nobody and M&M of Redneck Engineering; Dave Nichols, Scott McCool, and Jeff Moore of *Easyriders* magazine; Click Baldwin of Carolina Harley-Davidson; Terry Mac Campbell; Chris Maida of *American Iron* magazine; Tex and Critter of TexEFX; Wayne Springs; Jimmy Springs; Margorie Kleiman; Pam Proctor; Katie Putnum; Barb Wilson; Lindsey Beattie; Sheri Tashjian Vega; Jennifer Marquart, for making me look good.

And special thanks to all the great hot rodders and bikers whose pride and joy appears in this book. And also to the many painters and artists who paint these amazing works of art.

Foreword

The Custom Paint Code of the West– *By Keith Ball*

The terms freedom and freedom of expression are constantly in a state of comprehensive flux. In Tom Brokaw's book *The Greatest Generation* he speaks of the desire of 1940s Americans to free the world of society's criminals. The people of the United States did just that and rushed to battle in Europe and Asia. We were hell-bent to make the world right and free. At the time, freedom still remained a reasonably simple concept. We wanted jobs, education, and the right to religious freedom.

In the 1950s and 1960s freedom became a remarkably complex concept for young men who escaped Korea and Vietnam, returned to America, and expressed themselves ecstatically through rock 'n' roll, hot rods, choppers, and their colorful glistening finishes. The knockout side of freedom of expression was the ability to express oneself in any illustrious form.

Suddenly we confronted a rainbow of quests like the human race never faced before. We were truly free. Education was available for everyone. Anyone could seek any job or profession. Americans could travel most everywhere in the world and felt a God-given right to do so.

Creative sorts such as Ed Roth, David Mann, George Barris, Joe Bailey, Larry Watson, Bill Hines, Joe Anderson, and Jon Kosmoski rushed toward freedom of expression with arms open wide. To so many, including myself, freedom represented an artistic unbinding. I escaped the bounds of my parents, organized educational institutions, and the chains of the mighty military to build anything I wanted, paint it outrageous colors, and then ride it at 100 miles per hour or more all across the country. What could be better?

"Custom painting began in Mexico," Jon Kosmoski told me, "where they painted horse-drawn carts and stalls with bright colors for festivals." Color represented a celebration of life and the art crept north into Southern California and spread across the country. Jon experimented with lacquer paints that cracked but were easy to work with. "We were stuck with iron-based pigments and the colors were lackluster and dull. I met Dr. Palmer and we worked with expensive man-made organic pigments for more brilliant hues."

Joe Bailey invented the first candy colors in 1953 in San Francisco, and the industry went wild. In 1953 Jon painted his first motorcycle. All Honda's were shipped to the U.S. painted gray. "I asked the local dealer for a set of new-bike sheet metal. I painted it some wild crimson metallic and the bike sold in 20 minutes. They tore all the sheet metal off all their new models and suddenly I was a production custom painter."

Phil Stadden, a painter in Los Angeles, grew up making deliveries for his father's Dupont Automotive Paint Shop. "I was so fortunate to be able to roam into the back of hot rod shops where they laid out the graphics on dragsters, pinstriped flames on hot rods, and I watched them spray candy-apple red for the first time. I was 13 in 1962, and all the local painters enjoyed demonstrating their techniques to me."

His dad gave him a brand new spray gun and all the supplies he needed to get started. "My first paint job was a set of flat tan shop-truck wheels for my dad," Phil said. "They were plain, but we started painting wheels candy colors to add a custom touch to any car, then we metal-flaked car roofs

Aztec Gold. It took coat after coat of nitrous cellulous clear. We were just spraying clear over jagged glitter."

Freedom of expression was reached on myriad different paths. Jon studied the chemical production side, Phil had his dad's support and industry insider training, and a young artist in the northwest had an illustrator's talent and fought for the opportunity to learn painting techniques. "I was kicked out of every paint shop," Tim Conder said. They thought I could draw, but I had no painting experience or talent. I was brought up to respect my elders so I succumbed and went home, but I kept trying. I wanted to paint metalflake so bad."

He met a wealthy gentleman with a passel of old Harleys. The owner allowed him to paint one of his bikes, "You can do it," he told Tim.

"I did, when I was 28, in 1992, and he still owns that bike," Tim said. "I rented a paint booth, did the work, and when I was done, the paint shop owner was jealous and kicked me out." He painted it Hawaiian Orchid purple pearl with Lapis blue pinstriping and orange, yellow, and red traditional flames.

Tim finally painted bikes for Russ Tom and his rich client on Elliot Avenue in Seattle at night. "I lived in the garage," Tim said, "so I painted them on the street after traffic and rolled 'em inside to cure."

Jon Kosmoski, the man behind House of Kolors, watched the art change dramatically over the years as the chemists developed improved toners, clear coats, and pigments. They wrestled from nitrous cellulous lacquers and dull colors to acrylic lacquers and then urethanes in 1965. The movement expanded to acrylic lacquers that lasted and were crack resistant, then acrylic enamels were even more durable, and hardener was used. Urethanes became available in 1965 and delivered the workability of lacquer and extreme durability. "They didn't crack or scratch and lasted forever." But urethanes were tough on the EPA concerns and the users.

Now the industry faces one more obstacle to freedom with legislative demands to use water-based paints. "Water-based top coats won't be available for another ten years," Jon said. Primers can't be water based until they invent a way for water not to induce metal corrosion, by merging it with a solvent.

In the wild 1950s it all exploded in metal flake luster and candies. Then acid-trip metallics transcended the 1960s to be refined in the 1970s and 1980s only to be restricted in the 1990s. Right now we face freedom in a mirror of restriction and try to balance the two, hopefully with respect for both endeavors, creative freedom and global longevity.

What a wild road from black cars and flat army green to 360 supernatural brilliant SKUs in the House of Kolor Catalog and 30 new color hues coming on line each year.

I don't think many custom bike painters thought of our freedoms as they taped off their most recent dazzling graphic endeavor. But somewhere in the back of each chopper, hot rod, or other wild classic ride, under the gray primer and bondo, is a base of Freedom. May the Code of the West maintain its delicate stability and make it last as long as the best urethane clear endures.

Keith "Bandit" Ball has been deeply involved in the motorcycle industry for over 35 years. He is a former editor of **Easyriders** *magazine, former executive vice-president and editorial director of Paisano Publications and their 14 magazines, and one of the foremost authorities on custom motorcycles. He is currently working on the construction of what he hopes will be "The World's Fastest Panhead" motorcycle.*

1 This is where an idea starts, with the vehicle to be painted. Here is the motorcycle that is the subject of this story.

Introduction

The Journey of an Idea

The parts came to me with the simplest of instructions: paint it orange and gold. Sound easy? Not really. This was not just a custom-built bike; it was a show bike as well as a riding bike. The paint had to be eye-catching as well as durable. It would be entered in an annual bike show where my paint had won a major award for the past nine years. It was also a bike that my husband had built. So not only did I have to win a bike show, I also had to keep a customer happy, and there was my husband and his boss to satisfy. Plus, all their friends would be watching and "judging" the finished result of this bike.

Now, add the fact that I had less than two months to accomplish this miracle. That is six weeks from bare metal to clearcoat finish. Several of the weeks would be spent on body-work for the frame and sheet metal. That was the easy part. And during

that process, I began to think of the orange color I would use. The main feature of this paint would have to be the color itself, as there would not be much time for the artwork.

The bike had many round curves and surfaces, and I needed a base color that would take full advantage of them. I began to sift through color chip catalogs and realized I would need to custom mix a pearl color for the base, then layer a transparent candy color over it. I tested three versions of the color on a spare fender, and then plunged on to the parts.

The candy layers would be the hardest. The reason? As the frame gets coated from so many different angles, it is very easy for the paint to run, and some areas get darker than others. Often the frame will get darker than the sheet metal. Due to the extreme lightness of the orange pearl base, any of these factors—one run, one streak, a too-dark frame— would result in me having to wait a

2 This is where a design drawing starts. First I take a photo of the bike and use Photoshop to "color" in the frame. Now, the color is not correct but it's close enough for my purposes.

3 Here is the drawing I came up with. Not bad. Drawings are meant to give an idea of how the design will work on the vehicle. That is, it helps you know if the paint is on the right track.

day, and then resand everything and start again from primer. It was, without a doubt, the most difficult color I had ever sprayed. Each time I went to pull back on that gun trigger, I stopped to think and plan each stroke of the gun. And I kept wondering, "Will the end result be worth all I'm putting into it?"

Three hours later, when I came out of the booth, I held my SATA Mini-Jet 4 spray gun triumphantly in the air, yelling "Yes!"

Now I had to come up with a graphic that was worthy of such an incredible color. I spent a day drawing up designs until I finally picked one and worked on it most of the day. I wasn't sure I liked it, but the clock was ticking as the bike show crept up day by day. I spent the next two days trying to pick or mix

a gold to go with the orange. Every gold I tried looked just awful when painted alongside the orange. I made so many samples, I used up most of the areas on my original orange sample piece. In pure desperation, I mixed two of the golds together and went with that mix, even though I wasn't happy with it.

Now for the design. I had planned on doing gold panels over the orange, and it looked pretty good on paper. In reality, it looked hideous; plus, the gold paint had wrinkled. Panic set in. I started to sand off the panels, and then, when I was just about finished, I realized, they didn't look half-bad. "Hmm," I thought. "Maybe I could still pull this off."

I resprayed the panels, but this time I only sprayed around the edges, fading the gold into the

4 I had no clue my idea would work this well or have as much impact as it did.

5 Sometimes the best paint jobs are results of mistakes. But the color here was no mistake. I tried very hard for the "glow" that this orange pearl displays.

orange in the center of the panels. That looked better, but still not anything remotely close to amazing. But I kept trudging forward and began to apply a tribal design that slashed across the panels.

I didn't know whether I should say "To hell with it, it's going to be awful anyway" and save time by doing the tribal design in black, or if I should take the time to create the tribal in variegated red gold leaf. I did the latter, and was completely shocked when I was done. The various tones of the gold in the leaf brought together the orange base and gold panel colors and made them work very effectively. I began to smile. "I might just pull this off," I thought.

The day of the bike show was

bearing down on my husband and me like a freight train with no brakes. But I took the time to carefully lay down a very thin black pinstripe around the gold leaf tribal.

After the final clear was applied, I was stunned beyond belief. It was, without a doubt, the most amazing paint job I had ever done. The orange base glowed as though there were a light shining through it. The graphic had a traditional yet twisted mood to it that brought out the best aspects of the bike's design.

It went on to win First Place against very stiff competition. Against all the odds, time constraints, and color and design problems, I had somehow succeeded. Was it all my years of experience, my talent, or just plain luck? Or did all of those things contribute in some way to the end result?

I used to wonder where artists got their custom paint ideas. The painting part is easy compared to coming up with the idea. When I started painting, some ideas were easy for me. For example, with murals I would just go outside and take a few pictures, look at some nature books, dream a little, then arrange them to fit on a fender. For flames, I studied how other artists had done flames, picked the styles that appealed to me, and applied my own ideas.

Graphics were the hardest thing for me. I painted for 16 years and the thought of doing graphics filled me with dread. Artists like Dawne Holmes made it look so easy. How did she come up with those incredible lines that gracefully danced around the curves of a bike tank and fender? Andy Anderson of Nashville was another artist whose vision of color and form mystified me. And Bill Streeter of Connecticut regularly produced custom paint that was beyond anything I could ever hope to come close to. Where did he get those off-the-wall ideas?

It would not be until 2003, 24 years after I painted my first bike tank, that I would be able to come up with graphic ideas that I felt good about.

So where do great paint ideas come from? They come from everywhere. I get a lot of ideas from looking at magazines, looking out at the world, looking everywhere. Sometimes a great idea can come from the most unexpected place: a wild color in a fashion magazine, an evil design in a tattoo, a lonely road in the desert. Elements from here and there come together to combine and create something extraordinary. And that is what custom painters

6 The artistic mastery of Dawne Holmes is nothing short of amazing. Bike by Paul Yaffe.

and artists do: use what they know to make the customer's vehicle stand out in a crowd. Yet the best resource I have ever found are pictures I take at shows. Over the years the photos have filled box upon box. Then digital photos began to fill up CDs. With this book, I am able finally to share that resource.

In this book, I'll be doing the best job I can to guide the customer, the artist, and the vehicle owner to obtain the most effective paint job for their motorcycle or hot rod. In putting together this book, I went into my vast photo resources. I've been taking photos at bike and car shows for the past 30 years. Some of the photos are new, some are old.

In order to look forward, we must be able to look back and see what came first and where we've come from. In fact, much of the painting being done today is based on ideas and techniques that were popular

7 This is the first graphic design paint job that I was happy with. It was painted in 2003.

8 Effective custom paint brightens up a drab Las Vegas alley. Black Chevy pickup by Count's Kustoms.

over 30 years ago. Jon Kosmoski, founder of House of Kolor, recently talked with me about how widespread custom painting has become, with cutting-edge stuff, old-style retro designs, and new paint designed to look as if it were done 40 years ago.

So sit back on a comfy chair or couch, and grab your favorite beverage, because I'm about to take you on a ride—a ride through countless car and bike shows. Whenever I can, I list the name of the artist who painted the various creations, but since many of these photos were taken at shows, I can only show the picture and explain why I think that paint is special. I hope this book serves as a tribute to all the wonderful artists and painters working today.

I also hope this book helps the millions of custom bike and custom car owners out there who are looking for the right identity for their ride. A custom paint job can cost thousands of dollars. And if you do it yourself, it translates into hours of hard work, making mistakes and starting over, and buying hundreds of dollars in paint and tools. Use this book as a starting point. If you are inspired by anything you see, use it to create your own unique work of art. Or bring it to your local paint shop and tell them what you like about it. Don't copy anyone else's work. Sometimes studying another artist's technique can help a person figure out how it was done.

Let this book lead you on a journey of your own, a journey that may be created across the metal skin of your own beloved ride.

1 Two stock bikes. Which one stands out more? Do you even notice the one with stock paint and only chrome bolt-on parts?

What Makes a
Great Paint Job?

Author's Note: This book has a good deal of eye candy in it, but please don't ignore the first few chapters. Get it over with—savor the eye candy chapters, then come back and read the first five chapters. There's a lot of good information in them that will save you some grief down the road. Don't wait until after you've made a big mistake.

Why Custom Paint?
Take two bikes, both stock from the dealership floor, looking like all of the other thousands of bikes that rolled off the assembly line. On one bike we install high-dollar custom wheels with matching pulleys and rotors and throw in some new tires for those wheels. Of course, we'll need some custom brake calipers. But as you look around the dealership there are all kinds of sweet shining chrome doodads that can replace all those ugly stock parts. The bill can really add up, sometimes exceeding $3,000, easily. But what if you spent that same amount on custom paint?

Custom paint personalizes your ride in a way that bolt-on parts never

2 The owner of this 1939 Ford loved it. But he did not have much company in that opinion. Is this just an awkward body style no matter what, or can the right paint job bring out a diamond in the rough?

3 Is this the same 1939 Ford? Yes, it is. And it won PPG's Most Outstanding Paint of 2006 award. It was also featured in *Street Rod Builder* magazine and appeared in a number of other car magazines. How was this accomplished? Take a look at the previous photo. The rear end of the car is so round and big that it overpowers the front half. The front half needed something to bring it out, and the back half needed to be de-emphasized. Black is "slenderizing," so the car was painted and the artwork was limited to the front portion of the vehicle. The brightness of the real fire flames gives a sense of symmetry and balance to the car's body style. The funny part is the customer first told me black was the only color that he did not want.

will. It makes a bike or car unlike any other, whereas chrome parts come out of a catalog and there will be many other bikes out there with wheels just like yours.

But then getting a bike painted has its downside. It is much, much easier to go into a shop and simply pick a part out of a catalog or off a wall. Simple, quick, no fuss. With custom paint there are many decisions to make. Picking a painter is just one of them. You need to be sure your paint is done correctly. Refer to Chapter 2 for more information.

But for many people, the big question is: What should my paint look like? There are many kinds of paint jobs on the road: the good, the average, the absolutely incredible, and the just plain bad. And the goal of this book is to help you design that one-of-a-kind paint job that you'll be proud of.

Is Love Blind?
Yes, you are quite proud of that motorcycle you just purchased, or that old street rod you just finished restoring. Its style is beyond perfection. But is it really? Does it

have weak points? Take a look at the following photos.

Stand back and take a look at your vehicle. Be very honest and subjective. Just what do you want to accomplish? Are you looking for sleek and subtle? Want to make that car or bike look like it's a mile long? Or do you want your vehicle to shout out, "Hey! Look at me!"

The Job of Custom Paint
Custom paint has one main purpose: to make the vehicle look good. The problem is that most custom vehicle owners have a color or design in mind before they choose their vehicle. And unless they have some real-world experience in picking out custom paint, there's a good chance they won't make the best paint decision for their vehicle. So to begin with, let's go over a few rules for newcomers, as there are a number of things that are guaranteed to create painting disasters and untold days of nightmare stress.

The Rules for First-Timers and People Who Dislike Stressful Painting Situations
1. Don't get an attitude. There's nothing wrong with being a first-timer. The biggest mistake you can make is to assume that just because you've read a gazillion car or bike magazines that you're an expert. Knowledge is power! Most custom painters will admit that they're always learning something new.

2. Beware of the all-knowing "experts." Listen only to people with serious experience. Opinions are like mouths. Everyone has one. And some people love to hear themselves talk. They will offer up opinions on everything from what brand of paint to use ("Real painters only use Triple XXX Paint!"), the right artwork ("Oh, flames are so last year—no one's painting flames on their cars this year."), or what painter to use or what price to pay ("John Doe is way too expensive; only a fool would go there. Go see Jack Squat instead.").

Make your own decisions. Do research on various kinds of paint. If you see a car with a cool color on it at a car show, ask the owner who painted it and what kind of paint it is. Observe how the paint is holding up. See Chapter 2 for more information.

3. Take your time! Unless the doctor has given you six months to live, do not rush the paint step of your car, bike, or truck project. I should have listed this as the number one rule, as it is the biggest mistake. And all too often the local bigmouth, I mean, expert, will feel it's his responsibility to tell you, "Waxhaw Creek Custom Painting is taking six months to do your paint? That's way too long! Go down there and tell them to snap it up!" Mr. Expert does not even own a custom vehicle and has never held a paint gun in his hand. Does he know exactly what it took to get your car ready for paint? The kind of

shape the existing paint was in? Did it all have to get stripped off by hand? What was the body like underneath all that paint? Did body parts have to be ordered that no one had in stock?

Short answer: There is no set time a paint job should take. Many times a painter will have to deal with the effects of previous paint jobs. A good painter will deal with and repair all the problems that were caused by previous painters who took shortcuts.

4. And one more thing about deadlines and paint. Paint is the last step in the custom process. The builder or fabricator had all the necessary time to do their job. The engine builder had plenty of time to put together a motor sweet enough to make the "experts" drool. Then there was the whole "getting the parts" thing. Maybe parts took forever to get because they weren't in stock or they had to be custom made. Now, this is all well and good. So why, at the end of the project, are you rushing the most noticeable part of your project? Reread the first paragraph of this chapter. Look at the pictures. Understand what I am trying to say? I like to tell my customers, "You can hate me for a few weeks or you can hate me for a few years. It's your choice." Sure, there are painters who drag their feet when it comes to turnover times. But many times a painter will get into a project only to find out that it will require much more time than originally thought. So work with your painter, not against him or her.

4 Ben Jordan of Waxhaw, North Carolina, built this sweet Harley rigid. It was not the first bike he built, but at the time he still considered himself a newcomer in the custom bike world. This shovelhead was his third serious custom bike. A great deal of research, as well as questions to more experienced builders and painters, resulted in this award-winning motorcycle that graced the cover of *Biker* magazine. Graphics by Ryan Young.

5 This is what happens when painters take shortcuts. The paint on this Miata was several years old. The painter who did it did not properly prep the car. The surface was not cleaned and sanded thoroughly. This meant that while the paint looked OK, as soon the surface was worked, the paint cracked and began to flake away. There was no way the surface could be repainted without extensive sanding to remove all the poorly applied paint. What would have happened if I had simply painted over it? The application of solvents in the newly applied paint would have attached to the old paint and lifted it off the surface, resulting in bubbled paint that would then flake off. Now, is this something I could have seen when I first looked over the car and gave the price quote and time estimate? No. And I looked hard. It appeared to be a good surface. Only after getting into the job did I see what a nightmare the previous painter had left for anyone that followed. This is why painters run late.

6 This is what happens when a painter ignores the experts and outside influences. I had a very short amount of time to get this paint completed on NBC's *Today Show* Chopper. So I didn't play around with new colors or designs. I went with a color I knew how to paint and a flame design I was very experienced with. But I chose the most outrageous color I use: Crystal Orange Pearl Candy. I designed this color myself. Note how the color emphasizes the lines and style of the bike. Plus, I went with varigated gold leaf, a nontraditional material for the flame. This is what is meant by effective use of color and design to suit the style of the vehicle.

7 Notice how the orange works with the design of the rear fender and sissy bar? It brings a smoothness to the structure of the bike. Now, if those parts had been painted black they might look smooth, but the sissy bar would be less noticeable. The sissy bar complements the overall design of the bike, and the orange simply emphasizes this fact.

5. This last rule is a message for the so-called experts. Do all of us painters and builders a favor and shut your big mouths. Now, of course, this is pure fantasy, as there is no shortage of experts and they will never fail to offer their vast opinions, whether you want to hear it or not. Please keep in mind that if they were busy with their own projects they would not have time to bother you. Remember: This is your project and your money, not theirs. Do not listen to them. Do not let them get under your skin.

So What Exactly Makes a Paint Job Effective?

The keyword here is "effective." There is no one thing that will make or break a successful paint job. There are many things that factor into an effective paint job. Finding the right combination of color and design will bring out the best features of a vehicle. The next four chapters will discuss each of these elements in detail.

Another Bitter Dose of Reality

Can you look at a car and accurately judge what's under the surface? Painters use all kinds of tricks, such as looking down the sides of a car from a very flat angle and sighting down the panels, looking for any waviness. Some painters use a magnet to look for true bodywork. Those incredible paint jobs you see, like the flawless 1955 Chevy seen here, is not the kind of result you get in a week or two. Yet many people would look at this car and think, "What's the problem? Painting a car black is easy enough." Jimmy Springs painted this car.

Some cars look pretty good when the work gets started, then every bit of paint is removed from the body, all the way down to the metal. Once that is done, any flaws are suddenly visible. Plus, once the primer coats go on, anything you did not see before will show. Now the painter has to inform the customer that the job will take longer and cost more than previously thought.

This is the difference between a painter with experience working on cars and one without. The experienced painter knows to expect a nightmare lurking underneath that seemly straight finish. They know there is no such thing as an easy paint job, and 9 times out of 10, serious problems will come up. So they inform their customers at the very start what to expect. They do not give definite answers, because they know there are no definite answers when it comes to paint.

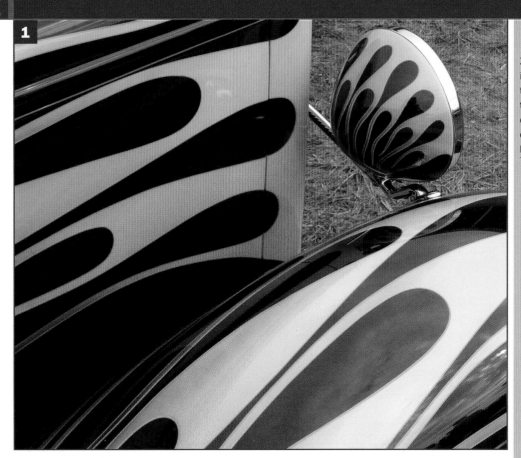

1 Looking for this degree of detail in your paint job? Be prepared to pay for it. It may be "just a traditional hot rod flame," but clean, meticulous results like this do not come from bargain shops. Flames by Wade Hughes.

How to Choose
Your Paint and Painter

So you can't paint your bike or car yourself. No shame there, but you can be an informed customer. Ask the right questions. What is their paint process? Do they guarantee their work? How long have they been painting? What kind of paint and filler do they use? Are they brands or companies you have heard of? Are you not very knowledgeable about paint products? Go online and do research. Hot rod and custom bike message boards are a great source of information.

A painter is different from an airbrush artist. Some artists are also good painters or they farm work out to a good painter. But there is a difference. Do not just go to the local body shop or find the least expensive painter. It will haunt you in the long run. You get what you pay for. Take some time and find the right painter for your bike or street rod. Ask around town. Ask the local shops who they recommend. Do they have any projects in the shop that the painter did? Can you see their work in person? Go to cruise nights and car shows and ask folks with cool paint. Give yourself choices. No painter close by? Go online and use a search engine to find a custom painter.

Most important, you want to see examples of their work. You want a painter with lots of experience. Someone who can show you many,

2 One of my all-time favorite paint jobs. It's just a simple but flawless gold flake paint that is only on the gas tank. The horizontal line of this classic Pontiac GTO decal sleeks out this Harley-Davidson Sportster tank. Sharp and distinctive, and it didn't cost a fortune.

3 My flamed chopper, seen here, was featured on the cover of a major bike magazine, yet I have put less than $10,000 in the bike. I beat out many $40,000-plus bikes at a bike show due to the detailed paint.

many photos of the projects they've painted. And not fuzzy photos taken from far away. You want to see close, detailed pictures. You also want online paint shops with experience in shipping custom painted parts or traveling to paint. Has the shop's work been featured in magazines? Has it won awards?

Take the time to carefully choose a painter that is right for your needs. If you have a bike or hot rod with a great deal of welding, choose a shop that paints a lot of bikes or cars with extensive fabrication work.

Know your budget and find a shop that can work with that budget. Remember, paint is the most visible thing you can do to your custom vehicle. People will spend big bucks on wheels and chrome but short-change themselves on paint. Bad paint is the worst mistake people make with their rides, as paint is the

last thing done with most projects. The money has all been spent on the motor, drivetrain, and wheels, so little funds are left for the one thing that will make or break a custom project. Plan your paint budget at the start of your project! Or else all those thousands you spent will go unnoticed at the show, with every-one looking at the low-buck chopper or street rod with incredible paint parked next to your high-dollar cus-tom with the low-budget paint.

The Ugly Truth About Custom Painting
Custom painting is not the smooth-est process. Things go wrong. Parts don't fit properly. Parts need more prep work than originally thought. In most cases, your paint job will take longer than you thought. So be prepared if your painter is not telling you what you want to hear.

Work with your painter.

Cruel Little Details

Patrick Kelly, the painter of this truck, went above and beyond in prepping and painting every surface of this truck. Even the sides of the tailgate are a work of art. This kind of attention to detail is not cheap.

Cars are not like bikes. They require an enormous amount of surface preparation before any painting can be done. And most painters really don't want to do all that prep. I don't blame them. It's hard, tedious, boring work. It is very easy to give in to the temptation and take shortcuts. So when researching painters and paint products, look at places where paint tends to chip, and hard-to-reach areas.

These include:
1. Around sharp edges of the panels, such as the ends of fenders, doors, hoods, and truck lids.
2. Along the bottom of fenders and doors.
3. Front and rear valances (the panels that

run under the bumpers).
4. Around the headlights and taillights.
5. Along drip rails that run just above the side windows.
6. Along window trim.
7. Around the grille and headlight area.

There can be many reasons for flaws in the areas listed above. Maybe the problem was that the area was not sanded properly. Paint will not stick to a shiny area, because it needs a tooth to grab on to. And it is very easy for the painter to miss spots around the edges. Many times they are close to the ground or hard to reach, such as the seam between the front fenders and the doors of a car.

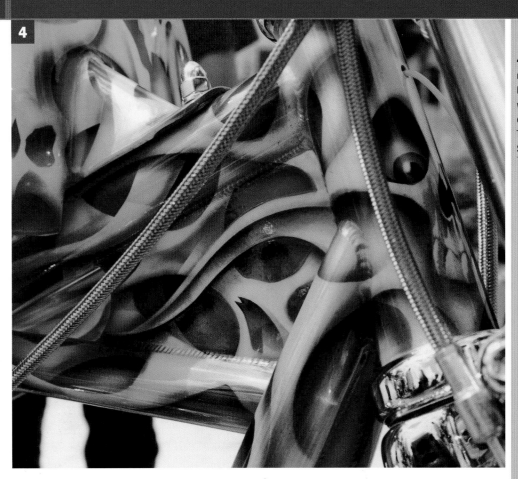

4

4 Look closely at the detail on the neck of this custom bike. You are looking at hours of tedious prep work and airbrushing. You do not even notice the welds on the neck. Time equals money. Artwork by Bill Streeter.

Not against him or her. You are both on the same side. The painter wants to do a job he or she can be proud of and one that will bring their shop more work. You want to get the best possible paint job for your vehicle and your money's worth.

When you are wondering why the paint is taking so long and call your painter asking why, make sure the painter knows that you want an honest answer about the reason for the delay. Maybe a previous job has complications that caused the painter to run behind schedule. Or a problem came up with your project and the painter has to figure out how to deal with it. This is not bad news. This could mean you have a painter who takes the time to do the job right. Do you want a painter who takes shortcuts just to finish the job on time? Shortcuts are never a good idea.

Bad news happens when you come to pick up your project and notice the ragged edge of the pinstripe around the flames. Or six months to a year down the road when you see the paint flaking off along the edges of the doors, or bubbly spots appearing on a fender. Take the time to get it done right the first time. And do not plan on having your project for a particular car or bike show, and then drop off the vehicle at the painter's two months before the show. If you have an absolute deadline, leave plenty of time for the painter to do the best job. And if the motor guy and the builder go over their deadlines and you lose paint time? Cancel your appearance at the show. There are plenty of car and bike shows every year, all year long, each and every year. It will not be the end of the world. But it will feel like it when you push your painter and end up with a nightmare.

5 Another of my favorite paint jobs. Four colors. Very simple. Very elegant. Very clean and sharp.

What Should a Paint Job Cost?

This is one of the most frequently asked questions I hear. There is no easy answer. Price will depend on several factors.

1. How much prepaint preparation work does your vehicle need?

Is it in rough shape? Lots of old, cracked paint? Dents? Lifted paint that has to be stripped off? Old artwork that needs to be removed? Rust? Fixing any of these things is no easy task and takes time.

2. How big is your vehicle?

The bigger it is, the more prep work required, the more paint materials needed, and more time to apply them. And while on the subject of painting materials, here's a very ugly truth. Paint materials cost big bucks. The days of $40-per-gallon paint are long gone. A quart of red basecoat will cost around $100. A gallon of urethane clear costs around $190. The catalyst for that clear is between $100 and $200. Remember, your vehicle will need primer, primer catalyst, basecoat, urethane clear, urethane catalyst, and reducer. And do not forget plastic filler and putty for dents and surface imperfections, and different kinds of sandpaper, from 80-grit for sanding filler, to 600 for sanding clear, to 2000 for buffing purposes. And there's masking tape and paper, plus fine-line tape for laying out flames and graphics. Materials for a basic single-color pant job for a car can easily add up to $800, usually much more. A bike paint job for a tank and two fenders might cost $400 for a single color.

3. What kind of artwork do you want?

How many colors? How many tape-outs? One set of flames will cost less than two sets. The more artwork, the more hours, and the more cost will add up. Do flames cost more than graphics? Does mural work cost more than flames? There's no one answer. It all depends on the amount of work done. This is why a customer should always talk about the budget with their painter and see if a paint job can be designed around that budget.

4. What painter should you use?

Much of the cost depends on the painter. A well-established flame painter like Wade Hughes will cost you more than the kid down the street who started painting this year. But with an established painter, you know what you're getting. Well-known painters have extensive portfolios and track records, they have been featured in magazines, and they have won awards. If you want the best for your car or bike, then find the best artist/painter for it. The biggest advantage to having an experienced painter is that they know what to expect and will price your job accordingly. When problems crop up (and they will) your painter needs to know how to deal with it. You're not just looking for a painter who does good paint, you're looking for a painter who knows how to handle painting disasters and knows the reality of what it takes to do a great paint job. Remember, the paint is only as good as the foundation beneath it.

1 These are really cool cars. But they all tend to blend into one another. Color draws attention to your ride.

2 Note the way the orange bike stands apart from the others. They are all beautifully painted custom bikes. I should know, because I painted them. There is an amazing amount of detail in all four of the bikes behind the first one. Actually, the first one has the least amount of artwork, yet the intense glow the orange pearl basepaint grabs your attention more than the other bikes in the photo. Color makes the difference.

Flake Paint

3 Flake colors are big flakes of reflective material that are mixed with clearcoat. They are best applied over a metallic basecoat that is slightly darker than the desired finish color. Flake paint comes in many colors. Candy paint can be applied over flake paint, richening the color and giving it more depth. Depending on the brand there are several sizes of flakes, usually medium and larger-sized flake. The tank seen here was painted with silver flake, then the scallop area was taped off and candy blue was applied. Bike by Stevenson's Cycle.

4 This tank was painted with a large flake that has a rainbow effect. Different brands have different names, like prism or hologram flake. House of Kolor calls theirs Kameleon.

Finding the Right
Color

I've gone to many, many car and bikes shows. Sometimes I'll look at a vehicle and wonder, "What were they thinking?" Gorgeous car. Lame paint. Dead, dull, yellow paired with dark, dark, blue. Good paintwork in the proper combination using color and design can work to a vehicle's best advantage. Color can make or break a paint job. This chapter is designed to help the reader understand how colors can work to bring out the best features of a vehicle.

Solid Colors

5 Solid color is a paint that contains a pigment and no other color additives like metallic or pearl. You cannot see through a solid color. While some solid colors are less opaque than others, they are not transparent like a candy color. Sound boring? If used on the right vehicle or in the right color combination, solid colors can be the perfect choice. Some solid colors do not need an undercoat. But some colors, like yellow, work best if a white undercoat is used, as yellow is not very "solid." A white undercoat can make a color like yellow or red really jump.

Pearl Colors

6 This mint green brings out the "pearly" effect of this pearl paint. Pearl paint is made with very little solid pigment. It is mostly binder and various pearl powders. It requires an undercoat, usually white or black. Pearl gives a soft, shimmery effect around the curves of a vehicle. Metallic colors are very similar to pearl, only the flakes of reflective material are larger and courser. A mint-green pearl is seen here on this Ford truck.

Candy Colors

7 House of Kolor's Kandy color chart shows each of their candy colors applied over various basecoat colors, ranging from silver to blue to red and green. The color combinations are endless.

8 This 1948 Chevy truck is a perfect example of candy apple red. Candy colors are transparent tones that are usually applied over a metallic base. The base can be almost any color. I tend to use candy or dye concentrates and mix them with clearcoat, using that as my candy paint. This truck also shows the result of very thorough prepaint preparation.

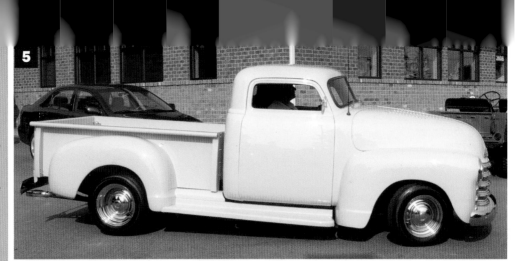

Factory Color Charts

Don't ignore the factory color charts. This sweet 1951 Merc is painted with a stock 1995 Ford color, Ultra Violet Poly. Al Baglione is the owner of this beautiful creature.

Marbleized Colors

9 Marbleized colors are fine pearl particles suspended in a clear fluid that is usually applied over a dark basecoat. Then, before the marbleizer is dry, a material such as plastic wrap is wiped over the surface creating random patterns. Marbleizer is available through House of Kolor and comes in six colors. Many times candy colors are applied over it. Here, a candy red has been layered over the marbleizer.

10 I painted several layers of marbleizer on this motorcycle tank. Then I layered candy tangerine over it. The patterns created in the marbleizer can be designed to complement the shape of the vehicle. Here I created vertical streaks to give the tank a longer look.

Color-Changing Colors

11 This Harley V-Rod is painted with House of Kolor Gold to Red Kameleon paint.

12 Color-changing paint is a pearl-style paint that changes color as it is viewed from different angles. It is available in many color combinations. A purple/teal/blue is seen here.

Color Layers

One cool effect is to have one basecoat color with a different color pearl overlay. Here, a yellow base has a lime-greenish pearl layered over it that only shows where the sun hits it.

Unusual Paint Effects

13 This is a very unique effect done with a liquid product that, when dry, leaves behind a crystallized residue. Here, a pink pearl basecoat was painted on the surface. The crystal product was then applied and dried. Black basecoat was sprayed over it. After the black was dry, the crystal residue was carefully wiped off, leaving behind this unusual pattern.

14 This ground metal effect is quickly gaining popularity. The metal must be carefully prepared by extensive cleaning. Designs are ground into the metal, roughing up the surface and providing a "tooth" for the paint to adhere to. A clearcoat, which can be tinted with candy concentrates, is then applied. This particular tank is a neat twist on a stock-style paint job, stock Harley-style panels and decals over an orange-tinted candy.

15 I stood around with several custom painters at a bike show, all of us trying to figure out how this effect was done. There are always new techniques being invented by painters who take the extra time to experiment and try for something different. A good custom painter knows the meaning of the word "custom."

Seeing Red

The most overused color for street rods is red. The reason? Red is a great color. But if every car is red?

Color Combinations

It's too easy for custom painters and their customers to fall into rigid rules about which colors go with another color. And remember, a single color can fall into many different tones—a red can be bright like a fire truck or so dark it is nearly black. A lemony yellow is very different from a school bus yellow. Color choices are a time for brutal honesty. If you have a poor sense of color and cannot tell the difference from lime green to a darker kelly green, talk to your painter. Ask friends you can depend on.

Understanding the Color Wheel

1. Hue: This is the actual color. Based on the color wheel, there are twelve hues. From top clockwise: Red, Red-Violet, Violet, Blue-Violet, Blue, Blue-Green, Green, Yellow-Green, Yellow, Yellow-Orange, Orange, Red-Orange.

2. Lightness or Tone: This represents the shade of the color. It constitutes the amount of black and white added to the particular hue. For example, pink is a lighter shade of red due to more white. And crimson is a darker shade of red due to more black.

3. Saturation: This is the vividness or intensity of the color. Deep Blue is more saturated than Oriental Blue, even though they are from the same hue and shade.

16

4. Similar Colors: These are colors adjacent to each other. Examples are Red and Red-Orange, Yellow-Green, and Yellow. This also includes colors with one color in between on the color wheel. Examples are Blue and Green, Red and Orange.

5. Contrasting Colors: This is when there are three colors between one another on the color wheel. Examples such as Blue and Yellow, Red and Blue, and Orange and Violet.

6. Complementary Colors: When colors are opposite each other in the color wheel, they are considered complementary. Examples are Red and Green, or Yellow and Violet.

16 There is no telling where a painter will get ideas for color combinations. This photo was taken in Washington State at the Spring Tulip Festival. A person may not think of pairing purple with orange. Or purple and green. Using a color wheel can help.

17 A color wheel is a very handy tool in figuring out color. Compare the color combinations in the previous photos with the color arrangement on the wheel. There are six characteristics in the color wheel that the painter or artist needs to understand.

Color Combinations Based on the Same Hue

18 These are colors of the same hue but of different shades and vividness. This color combination on this 1939 Ford is a perfect example. Both colors are the same hue, a red on the pink side. Only the top is a lighter shade with a darker shade on the bottom.

17

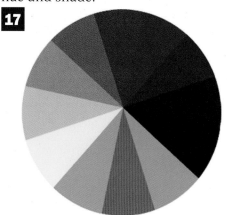

Using the Color Wheel

The designer and/or painter of this vehicle used a color wheel. The graduation of color from lemon yellow to banana yellow or orange to red or purple comes directly from the color wheel. Note the unusual airbrush technique. This fade is beautifully airbrushed.

19 Here the contrast between two tones of red is even more subtle. A red base with a touch of purple is topped with a red candy flame. The green striping around the flame adds contrast between the two reds. Green is opposite red on the color wheel and perfectly complements the reds.

Color Combinations Based on Similar Hues

20 As explained above, these are colors adjacent to each other on the color wheel. They have common characteristics in color, yet a slight difference between these colors can be felt. Here a red base color has been paired up with an orange flame. A blue pinstripe helps them play off each other.

21 This combination of purple and blue is a cross between similar and contrasting hues. The rich candy purple plays off the bright pearl candy blue.

Color Combinations Based on Contrasting Hues

22 Was this guy at the Tulip Fest? Two-tone 1949 Ford, orange topped with purple, separated by a teal graphic striped with lime green. An additional graphic, dark orange striped in light purple, runs beneath it. Note the soft black airbrushed shadows under the graphics, which give the graphics dimension by "lifting" the graphics off the surface. The contrast of the orange and purple is very bold. If bold and bright are what you want for your vehicle, then contrasting colors are the best choice.

23 This combination of yellow and magenta in between complementary and contrasting hues really jumps out.

Color Combinations Based on Complementary Hues

24 Purple and green are opposite each other on the color wheel. These colors bring out the best aspects of each other. Very easy on the eyes. That is what drew my eye to this bike back in the late 1990s.

25 Yellow and dark purple are nearly opposite each other on the color wheel. The painter may have to play around and test various combinations of these colors to get the best color combo. This bright edgy paint by Keith Hanson and Dave Perewitz uses passion purple to complement the lemon yellow basecoat.

26 Here again, purple and yellow play off one another to create this bold, harmonious effect. A soft orange fade softens the effect so it is slightly softer than the preceding paint job. Fitto did this amazing airbrush work.

Assorted Color Combinations

Pairing colors with black can create a striking contrast and be very effective for bringing out the best features of your custom ride. Vehicles painted with black have a more grounded effect unlike the shimmery feel of street rods or bikes with lots of chrome.

27 The solid red basecoat paint accents the sweet curves of this Ford truck. The black grille offsets the red and gives it attitude.

28 I saw this 1946 Chevy from a long distance and it drew me right over to it. Bumblebees did not come to mind, just clean and evil attitude. Keeping the yellow on the lower half of the car and trimming off the upper half with black accents the lower portion of the vehicle and makes this already long car look even longer. Sleeks it right out.

29 Candy blue sheet metal jumps out from all the black on the rest of the bike. Pairing black with color gives any ride a no-nonsense feel. Paint by French Kiss. Bike by Bill Dodge.

30 Can pink have attitude? It can when it is paired with black. Beauty and evil. The pink candy basecoat seen on this 1930s-era Plymouth is very rich and deep.

31 One reality of a great color combination is that you won't be the only one who is thinking of it.

32 Purple and black complement one another very effectively on this 1940 Ford. Not as dramatic as pink and black, but it's a sleeker look and more subtle.

33 Cream and candy russet gives this Model A a classic effect. Would the cinnamon russet work as well with silver? No. The silver is a cool color and would look awkward with the hotter tone of the russet.

34 On this 1939 Chevy, red and silver work together. The red is a not a fiery or hot red. It leans slightly toward purple and has a cool tone to it.

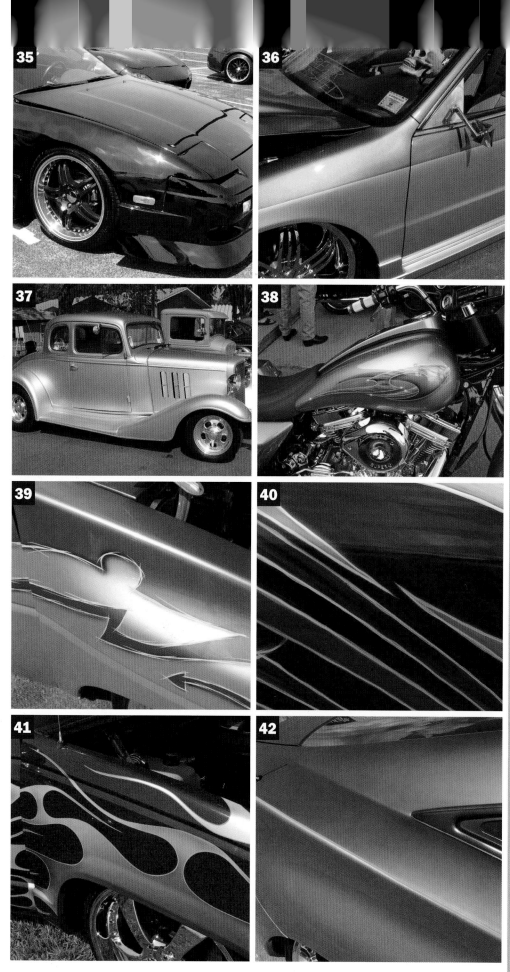

35 A black basecoat complements deep candy cobalt blue flames. Cobalt blue is a very "blue" blue. It leans slightly toward purple and has no green in it like Oriental Blue.

36 The silvery white page pearl contrasts dramatically against the candy tangerine. I don't know for certain how this paint was applied, but it appears as if the silver white pearl was sprayed on first, then the upper half of the car was taped off and candy tangerine was sprayed over it. The brightness of pearl white base gives the tangerine an electric glow.

37 This icy pearl silver and light blue pearl combo on a 1933 Chevy is pure cool elegance.

38 Another very effective use of silver pearl and blue. This is a "quiet" but effective graphic. Alone, the two tones of gray might be boring. But just a touch of blue tone brings it to life. Take a close look at this graphic. The darker gray is actually just some black sprayed over a screen. And the blue graphic was done in blue, white, and black tones that have been airbrushed into a stone-effect marble. Bike by Donnie Smith Customs.

39 This is a color combo I would have never thought of. A silver pearl paired with a silver green and accented with yellow. It works.

40 And silver with purple. A very effective combination.

41 Silver paired with red works great for these flames when accented with a lime green pinstripe.

42 Here's an interesting twist: Flat-finish gray combined with a shiny blue/silver pearl.

43 Can powder blue look gangster cool? It sure does here on this Blazer when paired with white. Brutally cool. Nothing lightweight about this ride.

44 This bike makes powder blue look good. The blue brings out all the angles and lines of the bike.

45 Now this is a proper color fade. The pink transitions perfectly into the blue. Subtle pink pinstriping adds balance on the rear section of this 1941 Chevy truck.

46 The warm brown tones on the wood panels of this 1937 Woodie complement the greenish teal paint.

47 Another case of good ideas being thought up by other people. The color on this car is more green.

48 I saw these bikes pull up and they caught my eye immediately. Something as simple as color combinations can make all the difference in how effective a paint job is. There is no way these custom bikes could not attract attention. Orange, purple, and magenta offset with silver and blue or red.

Painter vs. Customer Preferences

Orange and blue color combinations are not my favorite—although, on this bike they look great. In some circumstances, they do complement each other, and many people love the way they play off each other. I don't agree. This brings up the subject of painter preferences. Just because I, as the painter, love a certain color combination, it doesn't mean the customer likes it. Painters should try not to force their color desires on customers if the customer has something else in mind. What the painter prefers may be quite different from what their customer likes. This is why customers and painters need to communicate freely.

Finding the Most
Effective Design

Look at this photo. What is it that catches your eye? What makes it good? It's the paint on these bikes. But what makes the paint work so effectively? There are a number of things going on here concerning color and design.

1. The colors are extremely vivid. They contrast sharply against the black basecoats. The contrast causes the colors to jump out.

2. The flame design effectively fits the space of the tanks and headlights. Note the balance of color and the black background.

3. There is a random symmetry to the flame patterns on both bikes. That is, the size, shape, and position of the flames is similar, but not too similar.

4. The flame design flows with the shape of the parts. The lines of the flame pattern flow very naturally. No hard corners.

5. Can you tell both bikes were painted by the same person?

Most of the time when people look at vehicles with cool paint, they simply appreciate the way it looks. They don't think about what exactly makes it so cool, or so effective. What factors cause a paint job to work? Chapter 3 showed how paint colors work together—now let's look at how design can make the most of a custom bike or car.

How a Design Works

1 My personal opinion is King-style Sportster tanks are not attractive. They are squat and look short. It means that any design that is painted on them must try to de-emphasize these factors. This King tank was painted with a special tangerine candy pearl mixture. A dark color would tend to have a slimming effect on the tank. But the hot, bright tone of the orange has a glow to it and "thickens" the tank.

2 It took me a whole day to lay out the flame design. I really wanted to use the flames to make it appear long and leaner. Now it's not just a "squat bean" sitting on top of a motorcycle frame. I did the flames in variegated gold leaf. The tank color looks great with the gold flames. The flames look good. But something is missing.

3 Wow, what a difference a pinstriping makes. The striping does a number of things. It creates a clean separation between the gold and orange and creates contrast, yet it complements both colors. But what it really does is add length to the flames. The pinstriped tips only extend about 1 inch past the gold, but that makes all the difference and gives the tank a longer, thinner look.

Artwork vs. Solid Color

4 Is a custom car or bike as "custom" without artwork as one with artwork? It is purely a matter of personal preference. This 1942 Ford Hi-Boy looks very cool painted this fiery tone of red. But would it look better with artwork, like flames or graphics?

5 Here's a Hi-Boy with black flames and a wicked killer rainbow fade basecoat. Now these cars are exactly the same length, but the flamed car looks longer. Note the trim line along the bottom of the car. On the flamed Hi-Boy, it has been painted black and disappears. That, plus the flames, narrows the body of the car and accentuates the length of the car. The fade also helps this lengthening effect. The brightness on the front of the car makes the surface look bigger and farther away from the dark colors on the rear of the car. Flames by Wade Hughes.

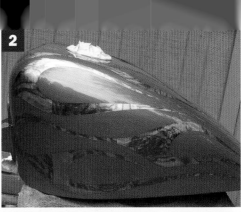

6 Now check out the graphics on this 1932 Ford Coupe of the same body style. Besides the fact that this is a very well thought-out and flawlessly executed custom paint job, it is very unique. As the lower section of the car has been paneled off in a lighter color, it makes the car look longer by drawing attention to the length.

7 Compare this altered photo to the previous picture. This Ford looks cool but definitely shorter than the other, yet it is the exact same photo.

Trying on a Design

8 This 1932 Ford is pretty sweet, but the owner, Raymond Mays, wanted me to spice it up. The overall shape of the car appears square in this photo.

9 This a Photoshop drawing I made after talking to Raymond. He wanted real fire flame, but just enough to complement the car. He did not want people to see the flames first and then notice the car. Compare the shape of the car in this photo to the previous one. The yellow on the front of the car seems to actually shrink it down, giving the 1932's form a more graceful shape. The car even appears longer. Prepaint drawings are very helpful and sometimes essential for finding the most effective paint design for a vehicle.

10 Here is the 1932 Ford after I finished painting the flames. It's the same car, but it sure looks different.

Same Painter, Different Styles

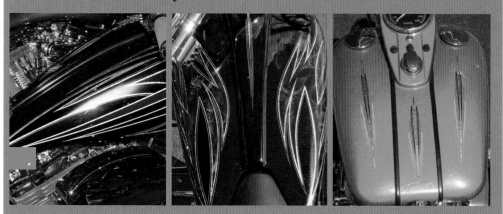

Does every painter have a unique style? Can you recognize a certain painter's bikes each time? Anyone who has been painting long enough develops a style. Look over these three photos. These paint designs are all quite different from each other, but they were all done by Dave Perewitz and Keith Hanson.

Design and Color

11 When the customer wanted yellow for this bike, I knew it would be a challenge to find the right color for the artwork. Yellow is a "glow" color and makes a vehicle look bigger, but in all directions... not just the length.

12 The angle of the design makes the most of the downward curve of the front of the tank. It slims down the tank and the gears make the paint very interesting. The paint goes from boring and bland to sleek and intricate.

What Is an Effective Design?

13 A customer sent me this tank with his old paint job still on it. The old paint did not work the tank to its best advantage. It was too round. The colors were too subtle.

14 They say black is slimming. It sure seems so here. The artwork cuts the tank in half, giving the illusion of more length. The black frames the red, creating contrast and in turn making the red look brighter. The design is limited to the middle of the tank. It is more than just a traight line, but it is still not overly complex. There is only one real curved line. The rest is straight lines. Paint by Crazy Horse.

Assorted Designs Based On Shape

15 Long tank. Long design. The tank has a square shape. Note how the flames are limited to the sides and top. This helps to keep the tank from looking too square. The flames help the tank look balanced. Paint by Crazy Horse.

16 This bike tank has a swooping curved shape. The sharp points along the border of the design keep it from being too round. The two-tone paint does the same thing here that it did in the previous photo. It gives a graceful mood to the lines of the bike. Bike by Grumpy's Customs.

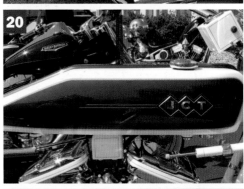

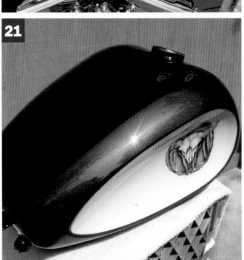

17 Now, here is a design that really emphasizes the line of this tank: bright, fun colors slashing across the dark background.

18 This a very short fender. And if it had been left plain black it would look even shorter than it does now. In fact, it does not even look short here. All you see are the flames. They dance very gracefully over the surface. The black also helps because the blue and green are next to each other on the color wheel. They are very harmonious together, but do not contrast with each other. The black provides the contrast. Bike by Redneck Eng.

19 This Donnie Smith custom features a graceful combination flame and graphic paint design. The design fits the shape of the tank very cleanly. The colors complement each other. A sharp and classic design.

20 Here is a bright white basecoat paired with a deep, rich candy blue in a panel, which fits the unique shape of the tank. This simple, classic paint scheme suits the retro theme of the bike. The white and blue are cool tones that give a sharp, clean effect.

21 This tank has concave metal panels on the sides. I painted these panels a cream color. The cream goes very nicely with the fire red candy basecoat. A bright white would have been too strong for the red seen here. But the cream would not have worked as effectively for the tank in the previous photo. This is the opposite of the previous tank, with warm tones instead of cool.

22 A very wide bike is slimmed down by a black basecoat and a long graphic that smoothly plunges down the top center of the bike. The soft color tones of the graphic keep the stripe from being overwhelming. No bright colors.

Designs and Trim Lines

23 A simple classic old truck. The blue color is very vivid and brings out the best lines of the truck. But the painter went an extra step and added a little artwork to bring out a very distinctive trim line on the body.

24 Here is a close-up of the artwork on the trim line. A very simple black stripe outlined with a very fine maroon pinstripe.

25 The old caddy has a very uniquely painted roof. It was done in two tones of gold stripes. Plus a color changing reflective flake, like Kameleon Flake, was either mixed in or layered over the gold. Very trick.

26 How to make a long car appear even longer. This old caddy is perfect for a lowrider-style paint scheme. It's a play on a traditional scallop design but with a twist. Check out the satin black finish.

27 Let's start out with very traditional yellow and orange hot rod flames on this 1930s street rod. The flames have a pleasant random symmetry. And no flames overlap each other.

The Hood Experiment

Everyone looks at vehicles at a car show, but it is impossible to accurately compare them. Vehicles are seldom lined up by design with graphics in one section, flames in another. So here I am lining up thirteen hoods. Are there any rules for painting flames? You would think so, but the flame designs are of all shapes, all sizes, and all different kinds of layouts. Compare and enjoy.

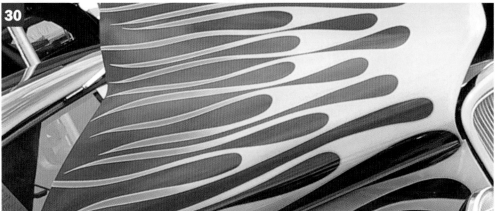

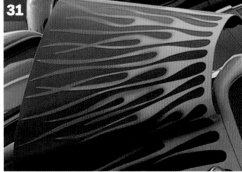

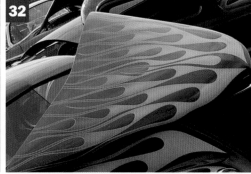

28 Here's one of the first car flames I painted. They are yellow and orange hot rod flames, but the way the base tapers is very thin. The orange fade does not extend too far into the orange.

29 Now, here's a sweet flame job. Wade Hughes has painted many flames, and it shows. Random symmetry, flame shapes that are similar but just different enough from each other, it creates a wonderful balance. Note the way the pinstripe is light blue on the top and lime green on the lower portion of the hood.

30 These are known as Ohio flames as painted by Bill Roell. Instead of the flame tails tapering down to the ends, these flames have a wide section in the middle of the tail. It is a very bold effect. Again, random symmetry and flame shapes are similar but just different enough. Note how the orange fade is limited to the rear section of the flames.

31 Hot rod flames done in yet a different style and layout.

32 More traditional hot rod flames. This time they were painted to fit neatly in the space of this V-shaped hood. Note the negative flame that comes from the very front of the hood.

33 These flames are a near mirror effect on each side of the hood with a flame down the center separating the halves. Yet you don't notice it right away.

34 Another mirror-effect flame hood, the same on both sides. This time with sharp, edgy, tribal flames. A great choice for this mini truck.

35 Simple flames. No overlaps, yet they pop off the surface. And they are mirror effect. The bright candy blue flame and light blue pinstripe has an amazing electric effect against the gray.

36 Candy blue mirror-effect flames and silver background that start with a cool graphic effect.

37 I saw this car at the Shades of the Past Rod Run in Pigeon Forge, Tennessee. Several painters commented that this was the best flame job at the show. Root beer candy basecoat paired with pale yellow flames and a fade from orange to root beer. It is beautiful.

38 A Honda CRX with flames? There is a lot of work on this hood. The flame shapes are very symmetrical, but they don't look boring or bland or overwhelming. They fit the space very well. What helps make the difference is that the flames start out as white, then change to yellow and orange. But the yellow of the flames is lighter than the yellow of the basecoat. There is also a very nicely airbrushed shadow under the flames.

39 This last hood is something a little different: a simple tribal flame with shadowed faces. More of a graphic than a flame.

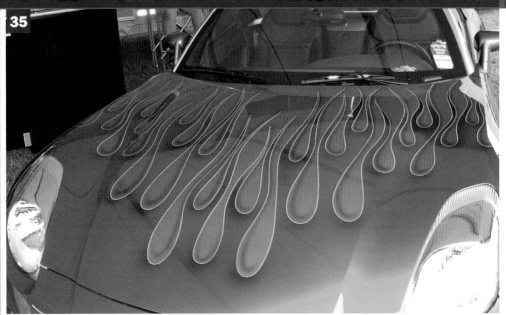

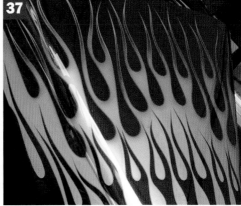

Used correctly, design can completely change the way a vehicle appears. Painters and their customers can have fun trying out different designs and finding the best one. The best method I have found is to make blank drawings of the car or bike and start sketching designs. I look over my extensive reference file of photos, pulling the ones that might steer me in the right direction.

Plan on spending some serious time playing with designs. There is no set time that it will take. Know this in advance. Don't be a week or two away from your deadline and expect to whip out a great design in one afternoon. Time is the biggest advantage you can have in designing your custom paint.

Color and
Design

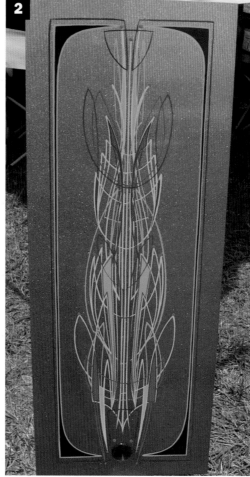

Color and design. Is there such a thing as colors that do not belong together? Colors that should not be used in certain designs? When you mention lime green to someone, most of the time they don't think it is a good choice for custom paint. As you look through this chapter, you'll see a lot of lime green as well as many other colors that don't seem right for killer custom paint. But pair the right colors together in the right design and you'll get some amazing results.

The Green Myth

Some colors get bad raps. Green is the foremost of these "bad" colors. But without green, custom paint would be pretty dull.

1 Good color and design should always complement the shape of the part it is painted on. This flame design emphasizes the point on this fender.

2 How about an olive greenish–gold basecoat with pink, powder blue, and lime green? It doesn't sound like these colors would go together, but judging by this photo, they look awesome. Jim Norris, a legendary pinstriper from North Carolina, made this very finely striped panel.

3 Lime green gold candy? It sure works here on this rigid chopper. But I knew I needed some purple to go with it. My purple flames give the lime gold something to contrast against.

4 French Kiss painted this Sucker Punch Sally custom rigid. French Kiss is well known for their retro paintwork. A yellow flake basecoat with a green candy fade. Very easy on the eyes. It's not overwhelming, and it has the right amount of brightness. The black frame helps to keep it balanced. If the frame were also green it might be too much.

5 Does this color seem attractive? Looks kind of dead. Would you paint your precious truck this color?

6 It was combined with a black basecoat, but it needed one more thing.

7 The lime green slash striping is exactly what was needed.

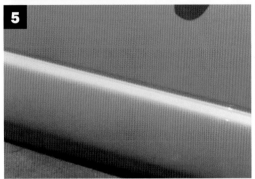

Billy Streeter

Most artists develop their own sense of color design. My favorite airbrush artist, Billy Streeter, has an amazing sense of color. He uses bright colors and lots of layers. In fact, the extreme color he uses is one of the ways to recognize his work.

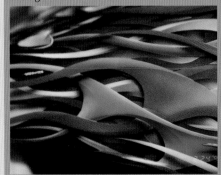

This is detail from a bike tank he painted. Endless layers of flames in complementary colors.

Pink, orange, green, white, and black. Unreal just how intense it is.

Simple but startling. A ghostly light blue flame, highlighted with pale yellow.

8 Take a close look at these flames. The bottom layer starts out white, and instead of going from yellow to orange, it goes directly to orange. This is a small but essential detail. Yellow might have been too bright for such a busy design. This bottom layer is stripes with lime green. The top layer starts out dark and gets darker. This creates a dynamic contrast against the white area of the lower layer, giving depth to the flames. Note the softness of the color fades. They are not very noticeable. These color factors keep this powerful flame job from being too overbearing.

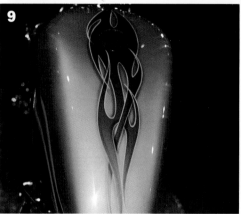

9 Very sleek. Very clean design. The green and orange are complementary colors and the green and purple are complementary colors. This creates a very harmonious effect. Put that together with the graceful tribal flame graphic and it creates one extremely beautiful paint job. Note how the graphic slices down the center of the tank. It is quite sleek and narrows the width of the tank.

10 Orange and purple again, only no green pinstripe. Actually, the multiset flames act as a great border to separate the two colors.

The Pink Myth

Pink is another color with a bad rap. Can pink be used without it seeming feminine? Take a look at these examples.

Using Color and Shape

11 Here's a truck with a flame graphic that works as a border between the two colors. The result here is an incredibly clean look. The white works great with the orange. It is interesting that the flame is done in pink. Yet, in no way does this truck appear feminine. Note the lime green pinstriping around the flame.

Color and design can also add depth and change the shape of parts. This is a long tank with flat sides, but this design softens those elements. The silver panel does not run the length of the tank and makes it appear shorter, more in harmony with the bike. The shadow under the red areas adds depth and shape.

12 Another amazing graphic design creation of Dave Perewitz and Keith Hanson. Yellow/root beer candy basecoat, incredible airbrushed arrangement of yellow, red, and green paired with a pink panel. The main colors are closely related, and most of them are next to each other on the color wheel, but the pink makes it all pop. The design complements the angles of the bike, creating flow.

13 Pink as a main color. This is more of a soft pink, a bit "grayer," or more muted. The color was pretty much dead until the flame was added. The yellow/orange hot rod flames provided a contrast. Note the way the flames are arranged on the car. The flames on the hood transition to the flames on the sides. Paint by Crazy Horse.

14 Again, pink as a main color. Minimal artwork and the slight offset of the artwork's location make it edgy.

15 Another soft pink pearl basecoat. It is nearly silver. It is a color so soft that it requires very subtle colors for the artwork. I went with a bone texture flame artwork that follows the contour of the oil tank.

16 Picture number one. Black tank with layers of blue and purple airbrushed flames. Paint by Crazy Horse.

17 Picture number two. A different yet similar black tank with layers of purple and blue airbrushed flames, only now a layer of pink has been added. Much brighter, but not overwhelming. Paint by Crazy Horse.

Good Ideas and Vehicles

18 If an idea is a good one, chances are more than one person will think of it. Here we have a bike that has yellow and orange areas separated by a yellow/orange flame with light yellow striping.

19 Now here is a car that has yellow and orange areas separated by a yellow/orange flame with light yellow striping. A little different, but with the same principle, and I bet these two people never saw the other's vehicle.

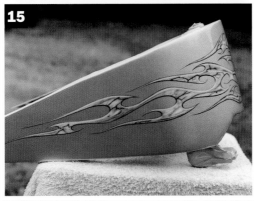

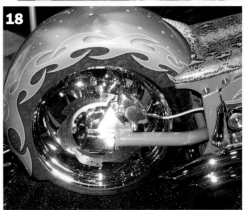

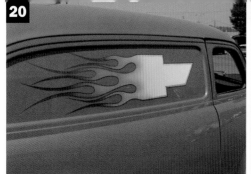

20

21

22

23

24

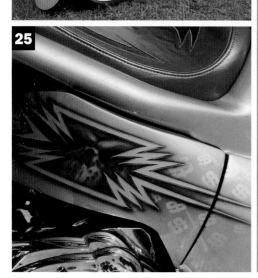

25

Slimming Graphics

One of the most common graphic designs for old street rods is to paint a design along the trim line on the upper part of the car's body, having it end at a graphic just before the quarter panel. This simple but very effective design can take a fat car, stretch it out, and slim it right down.

Fitting Designs into Spaces

20 Now this is a pretty cool design: A classic car company logo that transforms into flames. Note the beveled edges of the logo. This truck was so sharp with its deep, bright orange that it did not need much artwork. The design has just enough yellow, but not too much.

21 This V8-powered trike has a design that hints at what kind of motor it has. I love the way the artist did the checkered flag design. The realistic folds give it real depth. The design starts with a negative flame and ends with a positive flame.

22 Here is an unusually shaped oil tank, but Keith Hanson and Dave Perewitz use design, color, and technique to make the most of that unusual shape.

23 Black basecoat, full rear fender. Artwork that is a few shades lighter than the basecoat. If the artwork were a very bright color, it would overwhelm the surface. The monochromatic effect creates a sleek, elegant look.

Assorted Design and Color Solutions

24 Purple is great color. As yellow and orange are such perfect contrasts for purple, the combination is always powerful. Now this is a cool truck no matter what, but the brightness of the yellow/orange flames make the front end appear even bigger and gives the truck a more streamlined appearance.

25 A soft tan pearl basecoat. Candy root beer and reduced black are used for the artwork. Subtle, yet sharp and dynamic. The design runs from the oil tank onto the frame, giving the illusion of sleekness.

26 A fat fender. You might think red wouldn't be the best color for it, but the slim black flames dance across the surface, adding length and complementing the fender's shape.

27 Points on the back of the rear fender. As the fender is black, the points may fade into the black of the tire. But the layout of the flames draws attention to the shape of the fender.

Two Kinds of Scalloped Solutions

28 Stevenson's Cycle builds some gorgeous rides. Bikes so pretty they do not need much in the way of artwork. Here, a very simple traditional scallop design in a softly contrasting color to the bright basecoat is all this ride needs.

29 Another very simple scallop design, but done quite differently. An intense basecoat color is paired with a cream minimalist scallop. Just enough to emphasize the lines of the bike.

Using Very Minimal Color

30 A dark, natural-finish bike with no fenders, just the basics. Put a black tank on this bike and it would die right down. But with a simple orange painted on the tank, it all works together perfectly. The orange is very earthy and brings a warmth to the look of the bike.

31 Natural finish frame, natural oil tank—in fact, with the exception of the gas tank, every part on this bike is either natural finish or black. Since the gold on the tank is a metallic color, it flows with the bike's metal finish, yet adds a point of definition to the bike.

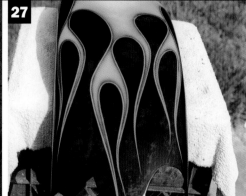

Breaking the Rules

Design rules were made to be broken. Some artists think that too much flame can overpower a vehicle. But Craig Kennedy's pickup shows how that rule can be successfully broken.

1 Painted properly, black is a wild color because it is so reflective. In the right light, it can look like black chrome, as it does here.

Solid Color as an Art Form:
Motorcycles

There used to be a saying that you could paint a motorcycle any color as long as it was black. I like black bikes. Both of my bikes are black, which may seem strange since I am a custom painter. But when painting my bikes, I have never even thought of painting them anything other than black. Granted, I did airbrush flames over the black basecoat. Does that mean they are no longer black bikes? Who knows? The point is, a bike should be any color the owner wants it to be. After all, it is his or her bike.

Can a man have a pink bike? Why not? I knew a very manly man who rode a pink chopper for a number of years. Would I paint my bike pink? No. But then I would not paint it orange or blue either. It's all about personal preference. One of the big arguments I used to get into with bike builders was that too much artwork would take away from the detail work of the bike. "Solid colors bring out all that detail," they would say. "Your eye travels around the bike, looking at all the little things they put so many hours of work into."

Some custom bike builders even have a rule about never having much artwork on their bikes. How true is that? Look over these photos and judge for yourself.

2 Look at the lines on this bike and all the sharp angles. It took many, many hours of fabrication and welding on the rear fender/seat area alone. A lighter color would have made this more noticeable, but the bike would not have the evil look you see here. Dark colors equal attitude.

3 Is it black chrome? You can see everything in the surface of this paint. The clouds, the sunrise, even the photographer. If there were artwork on this tank, you would not notice any of that reflection.

4 Gooseneck frame, peanut tank, Invader wheels, twisted motorwork. This bike is called ¼ Scorcher and the flake green paint complements these aggressive qualities.

5 Cory Ness built this amazing little bobber. I saw it for the first time a few years ago at the V-Twin Expo. There is a ton of work in this bike, yet it still has a very clean, uncluttered look. It's one of those bikes that looks like it's going 100 miles an hour standing still. The blue brings out this quality.

6 This is one cool purple. The frame and tank on this bike is unreal. There is so much work in areas that are not easily visible. But the brilliant purple draws attention to these areas, like under the bike. If this bike were a dark color, all that work might not be noticed.

7 Deep candy cobalt blue gives this already long bike a sleek look.

8 I do not know who painted this tank, but it is a perfect paint design. The trick was to complement the chrome trim. Flake base with green candy faded over the surface and around the edges. The tank works with the bike's design. It doesn't draw attention away from the bike.

9 I like unusual paint ideas. Here, the whole bike is black except for the tank. Even though it is painted a bright lime green, it doesn't look out of place on the bike. The Corvette emblem on the top of the tank was a great idea. I really like the look of this bike.

10 More gray and green—only instead of the sheetmetal being a different color, this time it's the frame. The green makes the frame stand out. This is one wild little bike.

11 Twisted Choppers built this bike a few years back. I loved the clean look of it. A chopper in its purest form is a bike stripped of anything nonessential. This bike is the definition of that statement. No artwork, no bright colors. Just pure brutal attitude.

12 Ironhead sporties rule. A bike doesn't have to be all polished and shiny to be "clean." Here, a red flake says everything this bike has to say.

13 More attitude, only this time with a classic no-nonsense attitude.

14 This is not a color I would ever recommend, but with all the gray and black tones on this bike, deep kelly green looks perfect here. Roger Goldhammer built this intense creation and he tends to choose off-the-wall colors.

15 This V-Rod has artwork on it, but I included the bike because of the way the color plays out across the bike. It is a House of Kolor Kameleon color changing basecoat, red to gold. This color is so dynamic that it doesn't need any artwork. And if artwork is applied, then it has to be very subtle. Paint by Crazy Horse.

16 There are times when it would be a criminal act to put artwork on a bike. This springer is one of those times. Black and white equals perfection on fat tires.

17 Fabricator Kevin builds evil brutal choppers. He makes sure to choose paint that will not take away from the attributes he desires. Simple, solid orange with a racing stripe on the top surface. Just a beautiful, classic chopper.

18 This is a mechanically detailed bike. Complex paint could push it over the edge. But this orange candy is perfect.

19 Another bike built by Dave. It can also be seen in the background two photos back. There's a great deal of clever engineering in these bikes.

20 The solid red paint shows off all the intense fabrication. Single-sided front end, one-off frame—unreal.

21 But what about stock-style bikes? Take a close look at this bike. Now, quick, look away and say what kind of bike it is. Road King? Dresser? No, it's a Sportster! The red paint makes it look bigger, since red has that glow effect and makes a small bike appear bigger.

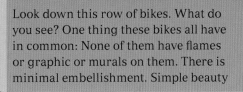

Less is More

Look down this row of bikes. What do you see? One thing these bikes all have in common: None of them have flames or graphic or murals on them. There is minimal embellishment. Simple beauty

22 What brings out black? A color that is lighter. A person can go subtle and sleek, as with a blue or green. Or they can go bold and bright, as with this yellow/gold pearl. It looks like there also could be a candy gold over it. One great way to go is to put down a yellow pearl, then layer a candy yellow or gold over it.

23 Not sure of the exact color here. Maybe a pearl-gold orange like House of Kolor's Sunrise Pearl? On a classic bike like this boardtrack-style sidecar rig, "simple" is the keyword.

24 The guys at Hard Knox never go for much artwork on their choppers, instead relying on color to make a statement. Simple pinstriping and minimal artwork allow this beautiful gold basecoat to shine and glow, making this bike stand out in any crowd.

25 Dave Cook is known for his unreal low-ride choppers. Leaf spring front ends, one-off frames, not much room for artwork. His solution is to keep the paint simple but very effective, like this gold/root beer candy. It displays all the elements Dave spent so many hours working on.

Single Color Fades

Single color fades are not used that much, which is surprising because they are a great paint effect. Here, it looks like a tank was sprayed black and a light pearl was sprayed along the upper edges and near the gas cap. Then a root beer candy was layered on top.

This is too cool. On the rear fender the pearl was sprayed around the mounting points such as the support/sissy bar mounts and the clip mounts for the taillight wiring.

26 Jesse Jurrens could have painted this bike any color, but he chose silver. A very sleek work of art.

27 Ben Jordan blew me away when he redid his old Panhead. Nothing old about this chop. And it sure didn't need much in the way of paint. Sometimes less is more.

28 Now, here is a real work of art. Billy Westbrook built this incredible rolling sculpture. Urban Hirsh is the owner. From the front of the frame to the back of the rear fender, it's all one piece of aluminum. No color needed. A monochromatic thing of beauty.

29 Is primer a color? Do all primer-finish bikes look "unfinished?" Led Sleds builds the baddest Sportsters on the planet. And this "primer"-finish bike looks anything but unfinished. Black and gray basecoat with flat finish clearcoat. Add a glossy black pinstripe. Smooth, smooth, smooth.

30 What about the average low-budget chopper on the road? Can it look killer good with just a single-color paint job? Look at this shovelhead and decide.

Ben Jordan

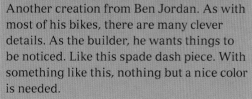

Another creation from Ben Jordan. As with most of his bikes, there are many clever details. As the builder, he wants things to be noticed. Like this spade dash piece. With something like this, nothing but a nice color is needed.

Solid Color as an Art Form:
Cars and Trucks

Paint color is probably one of the most debated questions that come up during a car or truck project. Many people will ask their friends, which only brings up more questions. One trick I use is to load a photo of the vehicle into a computer and use a graphic program to "color" the body of the vehicle. Once this is done, it is amazing to see the

various effects different colors have on the vehicle. Maybe one color was thought to be the best for that car or truck, but once that color is seen on the vehicle, it does not have the desired effect. This is why choosing a color should not be rushed into. Put some thought into choosing the color. Or else you might be going through the paint process all over again.

3 Would these cars look any better with artwork? Hard to tell, because they sure look evil with these bright warm colors. They really stand out. The yellow emphasizes the sharp, angular body style of the car.

4 This 1966 GTO is such a classic, and the orange pearl brings out the classic sleekness of the body style.

5 The headlight area of this car is beautiful, and the color showcases this. Solid color draws attention to little details that might be overlooked on a paint job with artwork.

6 Tubbing the wheelwells is a lot of work. Why hide it with a dark color or draw attention away from it with artwork on other areas of the truck? The bed of this truck screams, "Look at me!" It does the job paint is supposed to do: draw attention.

Seeing More Red

OK, so I said in Chapter 3 that red was overused for a base color on custom cars. But how could anyone say that red was the wrong color for these three cars? One thing these cars all have in common is that they have very curvy round surfaces and the red complements the roundness.

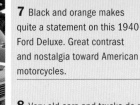

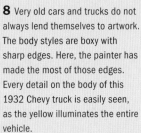

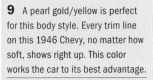

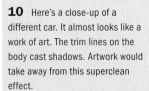

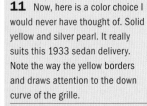

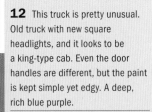

7 Black and orange makes quite a statement on this 1940 Ford Deluxe. Great contrast and nostalgia toward American motorcycles.

8 Very old cars and trucks do not always lend themselves to artwork. The body styles are boxy with sharp edges. Here, the painter has made the most of those edges. Every detail on the body of this 1932 Chevy truck is easily seen, as the yellow illuminates the entire vehicle.

9 A pearl gold/yellow is perfect for this body style. Every trim line on this 1946 Chevy, no matter how soft, shows right up. This color works the car to its best advantage.

10 Here's a close-up of a different car. It almost looks like a work of art. The trim lines on the body cast shadows. Artwork would take away from this superclean effect.

11 Now, here is a color choice I would never have thought of. Solid yellow and silver pearl. It really suits this 1933 sedan delivery. Note the way the yellow borders and draws attention to the down curve of the grille.

12 This truck is pretty unusual. Old truck with new square headlights, and it looks to be a king-type cab. Even the door handles are different, but the paint is kept simple yet edgy. A deep, rich blue purple.

Standout Colors

When a car or bike is painted a single color, you tend to notice the little variations of color. Artwork takes away attention from the base color, as artwork works together with the basecoat. When there is no artwork, the base color can show its best features.

13 Nothing like passion purple, a purple on the red side, to make a 1931 Ford street rod stand out. As there is no hood or front fenders, there really is no starting place for any artwork. The painter solved the problem by using a bright, eye-catching, nontraditional hot rod color.

14 The classic gangster car: Custom yet conservative rims and a soft purple/pink pearl color keep it traditional but not too much so. This 1939 Chevy almost looks like it rolled out of an episode of *The Untouchables*.

15 Dang, this color looks great on this 1937 Plymouth. When the color is the main feature, it tends to draw your eye to all the little details on the body.

16 There is a good deal of chrome trim on this 1938 Cadillac. If artwork had been done on it, this chrome would have been less noticeable. And with so many details, artwork might have made this car look tacky. As it is, the pink/purple pearl is very effective at showcasing the best aspects of the vehicle.

17 This fine 1946 Cadillac is much like the previous car. Classic lines, lots of chrome detail. Artwork would be too much for it. This simple candy red is perfect.

18 That is one busy engine compartment. And as there is no hood or side to cover the compartment, any artwork or bright color might overwhelm the car. A deep, rich candy like this red perfectly complements the design of this 1933 Ford street rod. The paint isolates and showcases it.

19 Soft teal pearl is a great choice for this 1940 Chevy coupe. Note how even the rear bumper is painted teal.

20 I saw this 1937 Ford from across a field and it drew me right in. No chrome, just a sweet, sharp blue teal pearl that almost looks like it could have some candy teal over the pearl. Or maybe it is a candy basecoat. House of Kolor has a product that looks like a cross between candy and pearl called Basecoat Kandy.

21 Here's a fat tire 1937 Chevy done in a similar color.

Same Look, Different Cars

Here are two car owners thinking along the same lines. Two similarly styled bodies, two similar colors. Both look awesome.

22 Look at this Nova Super Sport and just drool. Clean, clean, clean! This car could not be straighter. To put artwork on this car would be a crime!

23 Here's a painter who uses one of the same tricks I use. Get a color so dark it's nearly black. But where the sun hits it, it lights up with whatever color you desire. Here the desired color is a tealish blue.

24 Again, blue teal is a great choice.

25 If this little European truck were painted a dark color, not many people would take notice of it. But electric blue lights it up.

26 Blue is an amazing color. Here I cannot tell if the painter used a rich blue pearl, or layered a candy blue over a blue pearl, or if a candy basecoat was used. Good painters are always coming up with new ways of applying paint layers to get new, unique results.

27 Here's an interesting two-tone paint scheme on a 1940 Ford Deluxe: green body with black fenders.

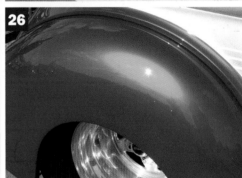

28 Green tends to be a more popular color for street rods than for custom bikes. This 1941 Chevy truck has a simple beauty. The rims are similar to classis 1960s-style hot rod rims but with a different look. Brake parts are painted to match the body. No chrome. Just a clean, crisp look.

29 Mint green pearl on a truck? This truck generated many positive comments at the 2004 SEMA show. That is what great color design does. While this color is not a common choice for a newer model truck, it works quite well. Custom paint is all about the unique and the unexpected.

30 A color doesn't get more solid than this teal blue. No pearl, no metallic, not even a drop of candy in the clearcoat. The only chrome is on the rims. It's an effect so stark, it's startling. And very eye-catching.

31 I was leaving a car show when I caught a flash of green glow from across the infield. At a car/truck show full of killer paint, this green was so bright it was as if a light were shining from it. Good color design does that; it makes a color look as though it were being illuminated. I'm not sure what exact color of green pearl it is, but House of Kolor's Limetime pearl comes close in tone.

Custom Mustangs

Here are three different Mustangs, two from the same year (1969) and a 1970 with nearly the same front fender. All of them have a pearl or metallic basecoat. The Mustang has great body lines that lend themselves well to reflective paint showing off these lines. They light up electric where the sun hits them.

32 A candy red so dark it is more of a burgundy. Look at the way the color accents the body lines. Color should play around a car's body.

33 Here is a Mustang with color-changing paint. The sharp angles in the body bring out the color-changing attributes.

34 And here is the same color on a 1951 Mercury. Looks good here too.

35 From a distance, this 1948 Chevy panel truck looks gray with a slight bluish tone to the surface.

36 But get near it, and wow. A sweet blue pearl has been applied over the gray. Back in the old days, we called this flip-flop pearl, as in sometimes you could see it, others times you could not.

37 Silver pearl is a cool color. Very sleek. If you're searching for an elegant look for your street rod, consider silver.

1 Classic hot rod flames. Never out of style. Paint by Crazy Horse.

Flames and
Motorcycles

People have been saying for years that flames are going out of style. I never bought that statement. Flames are cool. Flames are classic. Flames can be painted so many different ways that 50 years from now painters will still be coming up with different ways to paint them. To overlap or not?

Solid color flames or ghosted? Or both? Simple or complex?

Did I mention both my bikes have flames? Or that any bike I ever own with artwork will have flamed artwork?

I am not alone. Many people feel the same way. It's either flames or nothing.

So-Called Simple Flames

2 A single layer of flames, with no overlaps. Simple colors: black, flake red, and white striping. Yet it has a strong impact. The contrast is very powerful.

3 I painted this more than 12 years ago. It still has impact. The random symmetry of the flame shapes and the way they lay out on the tank is always attractive.

4 My customer wanted a red candy base with very dark purple flames. But the lilac pinstripe helps with the contrast and keeps the flame from getting lost in the red.

5 The shadowed dice design and the inset Harley-Davidson emblem makes this simple flame just plain cool.

6 A very thoughtful flame layout on this tank. Note the way the flames start up high and then come back on the tank, instead of coming off the entire width of the front.

7 The layout of these flames perfectly complements the angles on this Redneck Eng. bike. Note how the flames on the frame beautifully accent the flames on the tank.

8 Dave Perewitz is known as the king of flames. He has a way of putting together colors and flame design that is uniquely his. Yellow flames on yellow? Dave pulls it off like the pro he is.

9 Another Perewitz creation using colors that complement each other. Look at the way the flames dance across the surface.

10 How to paint a tank with a hole through it? With flames of course. Bike by Redneck Eng.

11 Something about this tank catches the eye. Is it the nearly ghost flames? Or the rainbow flake shining through the purple candy paint? Or the way the flames are laid out on the tank?

12 Simple pinstriped flames on a flat black surface. Great flame design.

13 Though not noticeable at first, there are shadowy skulls airbrushed throughout these candy red flames. The skulls were airbrushed before the candy was sprayed. The purple stripe adds brightness.

Accent Flames

Flames don't always have to come from the very front of a tank or fender. They can be laid out as a contained flame design that accents the shape of the part, as seen here in these two examples.

Solid and Ghost Flames

14 Bill Streeter combines incredible airbrushed flames with detailed ghost flames. Note the 3D edges airbrushed on the ghost flames.

15 Here Dave Perewitz does his flames and lays down a set of ghost flames over the solid layer. Same principle but completely different result.

Multilayer Flames

16 The unusually curvy flames caught my eye. It is also interesting that the top layer of flames is the same color as the basecoat, only outlined with lime green. Very striking.

17 There are three layers of flames on this chopper. The entire surface is covered. But it all works together and does not overwhelm. I had fun painting this bike, and it shows.

18 Another creation from the Shadley Bros. What's different here is that the flames are all located at the front of the tank. They don't extend over the whole tank.

19 The first mixture of solid and pinstriped flame paint I ever did. Many hours of work are seen here.

Tank Flames

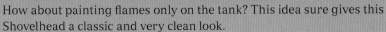

How about painting flames only on the tank? This idea sure gives this Shovelhead a classic and very clean look.

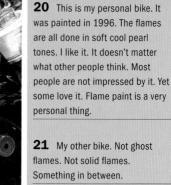

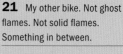

20 This is my personal bike. It was painted in 1996. The flames are all done in soft cool pearl tones. I like it. It doesn't matter what other people think. Most people are not impressed by it. Yet some love it. Flame paint is a very personal thing.

21 My other bike. Not ghost flames. Not solid flames. Something in between.

22 Simple colors, complex flames. The small amount of contrast between the chrome tones and the orange is very powerful.

Tribal Flames

23 Tribal flames have points where regular flames have curves. Black tribal flames play off nicely against an aggressive red flake.

24 First this bike was painted silver pearl. Then it was painted with gray pearl flames, and candy red was layered over it all. Finally, pinstripes were added.

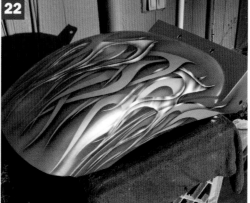

Tribal Flames

Interesting effect. Tribal flames were painted to look like they are under the basecoat. They are actually painted over the basecoat, and then shadows are carefully airbrushed.

25 It looks like white base was applied, then a rainbow flake. The brutal black tribal was painted, then taped off, and green candy was sprayed on the top half. It was finished off with a gold pinstripe. Pure evil. Note the black frame.

26 This is one wild little Sportster. Even the paint is unusual. Not your average tribal. This is what I mean by painters getting creative and coming up with their own styles.

27 Contrasting and similar colors provide brightness for these simple tribal flames.

Realistic Flames

28 These are more aggressive real flames, burning hotter. Real flames require a soft touch with an airbrush, very random.

29 Real flames are great for painters to work with, as images can be worked into the flames.

30 Realistic flames are simply flames painted to look like real flames. Here they are painted inside a panel on a tank.

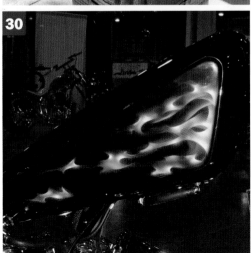

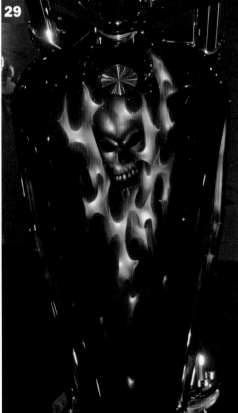

31

32

33

31 Real fire flames framed by traditional flames.

32 Real flames can be any color, like these smoky, mystical green flames.

33 Here, real flames are under traditional black flames.

Flames and Graphics

Here's an interesting way to start off a set of flames. This painter taped off an iron cross shape and then sprayed the flames.

34 It looks like there are only three layers of flames here. Two solid, one pinstriped. But it sure looks like more.

35 Redneck Eng. built this slick full dresser and flamed it with traditional hot rod flames.

36 Another Redneck bagger, this one with pinstriped flames. You don't have to have a wild custom bagger for flames. Flames would be perfectly at home on a stock bagger.

37 Sure, it's a radical custom bike, but picture something like this on a stock bagger. Notice the way the flame design fits the shape of the parts. Blue basecoat with light blue flames.

38 Stock-style bagger with a tangerine candy over a marbleized basecoat. And flames stretching from front to back.

Flamed Dressers

Most people don't custom paint their dresser bikes. Why do bikes with saddlebags have to be boring? Answer: They don't have to be.

39 The Redneck bagger seen from the top. Pinstriped designs run down the center of the bike and down the tops of the bags, mixing perfectly with the flames.

40 The trick to successfully painting a bagger is having a design layout that complements the lines of the bike.

Flames with Graphics

41 This is a very clever way to combine flames with a graphic. Start with a lime green candy basecoat, tape off a graphic with a flame or two, and apply a black pearl. Stripe with gold. Very simple, but very slick.

42 Obviously this saddlebag goes with the previous tank. The tank design translates very neatly onto the saddlebags. And by keeping the design low on the saddlebags, it gives the bike a more streamlined appearance.

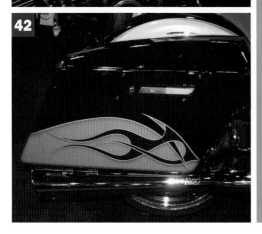

Subtle Flames

Several coats of marbleizer was applied to this bike. Then it was clearcoated. Next, silver leaf pinstripe flames were applied. That was followed by a few coats of candy tangerine. This remains one of my favorite paint jobs because I really love the way the light plays on the surface—plus, I enjoyed painting it.

43 This custom by Donnie Smith beautifully mixes flames with a very simple graphic, showing it doesn't take much to make a big statement.

44 Clearcoated bare metal with black flames. Add some evil old-fashioned pinstriping and stripe the flames with red. Unique and full of attitude. Never be nervous about pushing the boundaries of custom painting.

Flames and Murals

45 Look carefully at the tank on this Redneck bike. Note the forward angled slant of the tank and the inset matching it. The paint scheme fits perfectly and makes the most of the angles.

46 A skull with flames trailing off the back of it is one of the most commonly painted murals. Here is a version that I painted in 1998. Note how it is done in cool colors that tone down a hot color basecoat.

47 Bone-effect tribal flames coming off of bone-effect dice clearcoated with a flat finish. Another "something different" in the flame department.

48 Is it flames or a mural? Multiple layers of airbrushed flames by Fitto.

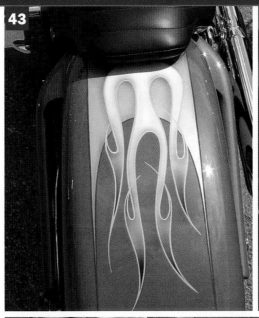

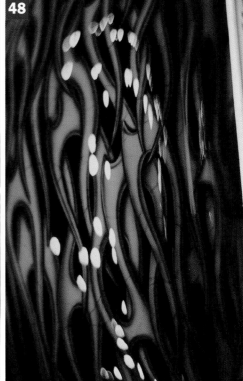

1

1 I don't know who painted the first flames on a vehicle. Flames have been around as long as people have hot rodded cars. People put flames on everything: toolboxes, chairs, refrigerators, doors, anything. Flames are cool. It is just as simple as that. This Ford was owned by John Booster.

Flames on
Cars, Trucks, and Street Rods

I don't know who painted the first flames on a vehicle. Flames have been around as long as people have been hot rodding cars. People put flames on everything: toolboxes, chairs, refrigerators, doors—anything. Flames are cool. It is just as simple as that. As to what style of flame? Now that is the hard question. There are many styles of flames. Many are seen in this chapter. Here again, making a drawing or digital scan of your vehicle and trying out flames can really help. Take a photo of your car or truck, make some color copies. Then simply draw flames on the copies. Can't draw? Just try doodling around with them until you get some inspiration.

Traditional
Hot Rod Flames

2 One of the most classic flame paint schemes is seen here. Red car with yellow flames, faded with orange and pinstriped.

3 Here's another street rod painted with the same style flame paint but done differently. That is the beauty of flames: No two are completely alike.

4 Another red street rod with yellow/orange flames, yet it is completely different. Instead of the flame coming off the entire front of the car, the flame is "contained." The flames start at specific points. More of a strip flame.

5 Beautiful red paint. Even the bumpers are painted, and it has a simple traditional flame strip.

6 Canada's Ron Gibbs, the Canadian Rat Fink, has his own unique way of painting classic-style flames, as seen here on this Ford Coupe. Observe the wonderfully symmetrical yet random flame layout.

7 This red pickup truck with classic-style flames is quite different from the others. The flames start out white, then change to yellow and orange. The white gives it a whole different effect.

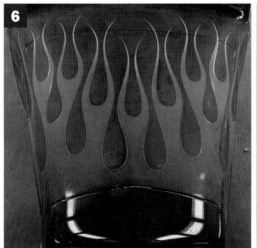

Flames on **Cars, Trucks, and Street Rods**

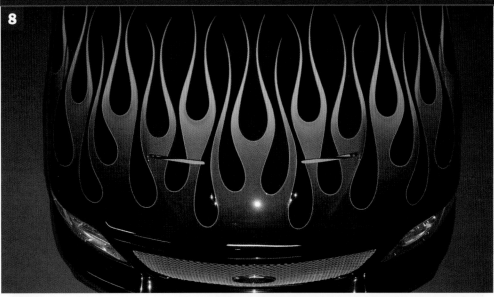

8 The Canadian Rat Fink's flames are so recognizable. Near perfection in a mirror image on each half of the hood. Note the reverse color fade, dark to light rather than light to dark.

9 More Rat Fink traditional flames, this time on a Chevy SSR. Whether it's an old or new vehicle, traditional flames are never out of style.

10 Take a stock black PT Cruiser and flame it. Instantly cool.

11 Now here is a kind of car you don't see flamed very often. But flames make it stand out.

12 Here, the flames are coming off of the grille. It gives this '48 a very unique look.

13 More uniquely painted traditional-style flames.

14 More incredible hot rod flames courtesy of Ron Gibbs, this time on a Ford truck.

15 This little open wheel is wilder with traditional flames.

16 How well do flames show up at night? These yellow hot rod flames are burning bright. Note how the flames start at the firewall.

17 Now, this is ultrabright. Pearl orange over a white base. Maybe a touch of candy tangerine mixed with the clear . . . white hot flames that fade to passion purple. So bright it pulsates.

18 A very subtle blue basecoat. But again, white flames that fade to yellow then orange add lots of spark.

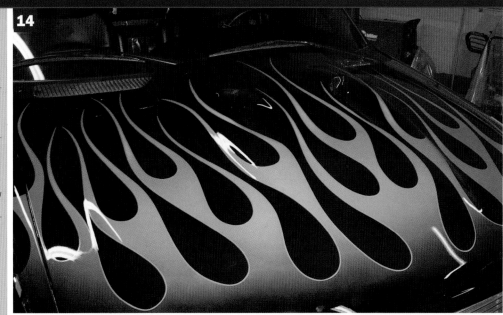

Flames on **Cars, Trucks, and Street Rods**

19 This car is beyond cool. Shaved door handles, no wipers, no bumpers. Classic hot rod rims. Pearl blue basecoat with ice silver pearl flames that fade to blue. Light blue striping. Flames don't always have to be yellow and orange.

20 This truck is called the *Blue Flame*. But unlike the previous car, the flames are a solid color, no pearl. This makes the flames stand off the surface slightly.

21 People are always trying something different. Traditional flames that come from two simple graphic stripes.

22 Frank Tetro's pearl silver '33 Speedster looks even speedier with candy cobalt blue flames. Flames by Joe Richardson. Note the lime green striping.

23 Mike Galarde's '41 Willys coupe is another silver pearl street rod with blue flames, but in a different style. Jim Farr painted these "Ohio"-style flames. More on Ohio flames coming up later in this chapter.

Custom Details

It's the little details that make all the difference. Here's the engine compartment of Frank's Speedster. The flamed valve covers are way cool.

24 Leave it to the Canadian Rat Fink to come up with flames that fit into a classic stock Chevy paint scheme. Notice the reverse fade, from dark to light. The tips of the flames are nearly white.

25 Another unique twist on traditional flames using similar colors. A dark green pearl basecoat with a lighter but similar tone of green flames. The flame color is edged around the border of the flame. Not a ghost flame but done using the same technique.

26 A dark burgundy car with minimal chrome. See how big the grille is? It stretches completely around the nose of the car, yet it is not noticeable because it is painted the same color. A simple strip of white flame complements the paint scheme.

27 A fiery orange strip of flame gives a different look to this maroon street rod.

28 No color fade on this traditional flame. Just a black base and a purple pearl flame striped with lime green. Satin clear finish gives this flame paint a truly unique appearance.

29 This is almost a tribal flame, as there are little points coming off the body of the flame. It gives this car an edgy feel.

Using Flames as a Border on Two-Tone Paint Schemes

30 Jerry Juden's '34 Ford Roadster is one sleek car. An intertwining strip of flame serves as a border between the two-tone Prowler orange and black paint. Note how the black extends around the grille.

31 How to do a hot rod taxi-cab paint scheme: Two tones of yellow with a checker stripe that turns into traditionally shaped flames.

32 Here's a close-up of the checked flame. Notice how the checkers are not straight up and down. They flow as if they were on fabric. The checkers flow with the flame.

33 Simple colors with a very uncomplicated flame suits this panel truck just fine.

Different is Good

Here is an unusual but very cool way to paint flames. Ron Gibbs painted traditional flames on the lower rocker areas of the body of this Chevy ProStreet drag car. The flames "frame" the red, emphasizing it.

34 Here is a narrow flame border, fitting neatly above the body's trim line.

35 Here's an unusual take on the flame border paint scheme. Note the warm colors, red with gold with yellow.

36 This is the most incredible vehicle I saw while attending a year's worth of car shows: a 1932 Ford bus restored by Williams Street Rods. It was basically a rusty shell when they started. The paint scheme is simply amazing. Wild, curly flames separate the tangerine pearl and black. Notice how the flame and bottom color are so similar. This creates a very smooth effect. Because the flame design is so wild, bright colors would not have worked.

37 The transition of the flame at the rear of the bus is pure genius.

38 A close-up of the flame design. The two tones of tangerine are just beautiful. Everything in this paint scheme works in harmony.

39 Two layers of flames act as a flame border here. Note how one of the flame layers is simply an extension of the bottom base color. Pretty slick idea.

40 Here the top of the bottom color becomes the flame.

Flames on **Cars, Trucks, and Street Rods**

Ohio Flames

41 Wade Hughes is one of the best-known painters of what is known as Ohio flames, which have long shapes and long tails that sometimes taper, then get thicker before tapering again. Here, he has painted Ohio flames on a Ford.

42 Here, he has flamed a purple convertible.

43 Here is a street rod with flames by the legendary Bill Roell, the custom painter who started the Ohio flames craze. In 2006, Bill was inducted into the National Hot Rod Association (NHRA) Hall of Fame for his custom paintwork. The green pinstripe is a cool effect.

Small Hidden Details

It doesn't take much to make a bold statement. This little flame detail on the radiator shroud of the engine compartment features Ohio flames and is the only artwork on this classic woody. It can only been seen when the hood is open.

44 More Ohio flames, with a very traditional layout.

45 Now, here are Ohio flames with a very unique layout limited to the tops of the front fenders and doors of this Chevy truck.

46 This '32 Ford Hi-Boy is without a doubt the sweetest flame paint I have ever seen. Wade Hughes painted traditional flames against a flawless rainbow fade. In most cases, the flames are lighter than the background. Here, the flame colors are reversed. Note in the yellow area the flame's pinstripe is green, and then it changes to blue.

Other Flame Styles

47 This flame is so slender that at first glance it does not even look like a flame.

48 But with a close-up look, the extreme detail of this flame can easily be seen.

Ohio Flames

The exact shape of Ohio flames can be seen in this close-up of the Chevy truck.

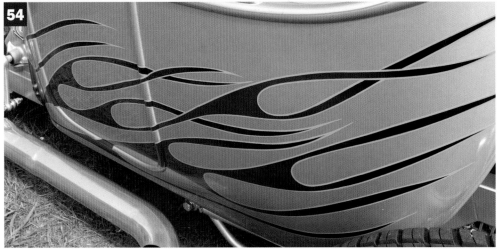

49 Flames can get very slim, like these simple but very slender orange flames. There is no color fade on these flames.

50 Photos don't accurately show how incredible this paint is. Just what was used for the flames layered over this very deep candy pearl tangerine?

51 Sheets of variegated gold leaf were applied as flames. Then it appears that a candy tangerine was layered over the gold leaf flames. The airbrushed shadows add depth. The flame shape looks to be Ohio style.

52 Here's a different flame airbrushed with a three-dimensional effect. Notice the beveled areas of the flames with the airbrushed highlights.

53 Can a T-bucket be flamed? Sure, here is a T-bucket with hot rod flames.

54 And here's a T-bucket with an Ohio-style flame. Note this is one of the few dark flames on a lighter colored base seen in this chapter. I did not see many flame jobs on cars with dark flames.

55 Another dark-on-light flame paint job. While the candy red is incredibly fine, there is an old-school rough-and-tumble mood in this flame paint.

56 And one last dark-on-light, this time a deep candy maroon on yellow. Look closely at the front of the flames. A flame shape comes out of the yellow. Very trick.

57 The flame job on this coupe runs along the same lines of the previous photo, but it's much more extreme. The basecoat flames at the front of the car act as an additional layer of flames.

Soft Flames

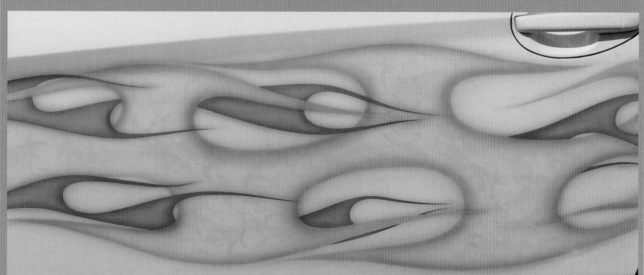

Painters are always coming up with new ways of filling their flames. The effect here is very soothing. Very soft, cool tones. In the "gray" flame, there are actual shark shapes airbrushed in the flame. This subtle effect is opposite of the usual bold look of flames, but just as strong.

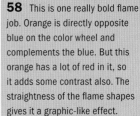

58 This is one really bold flame job. Orange is directly opposite blue on the color wheel and complements the blue. But this orange has a lot of red in it, so it adds some contrast also. The straightness of the flame shapes gives it a graphic-like effect.

59 Oh yeah, flames on a station wagon! This is pretty intense flame paint. Bright red basecoat with two layers of pearl flames in colors that are closely related.

60 Large, wild flame shapes dance playfully across the surface of this street rod truck. Yellow and orange are next to each other on the color wheel. If the flames were a contrasting color, it would not be as harmonious as it is here.

Ghost Flames

61 This is not a ghost flame, but it was sprayed like a ghost flame. A silver pearl was applied, and then candy green was layered on toward the rear of the flame.

62 These flames have some aspects of ghost flames. They are sprayed in soft pearl tones. Note the true ghost flame in purple that is layered over the lavender pearl flame.

Dagger Pinstriping

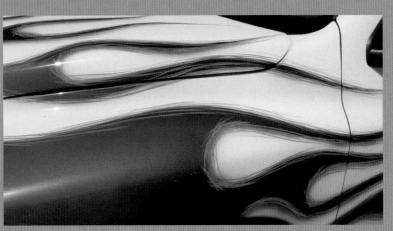

This is what is known as dagger pinstriping. Besides being very different from traditional striping, it adds edginess to a flame job and is an easy stripe to paint, especially for painters like me who cannot hold a smooth line.

63 True ghost flames are very hard to photograph. They can only be seen from certain angles and in certain light. Here's a layer of ghost flames on this '68 Camaro.

Flames as Trim Accents

64 One of the most common ways to streamline an old street rod is to run a stripe down the body's upper trim line and have a small, sleek design just past the end of the door on the upper quarter. Here, that design is an Ohio-style flame filled with a paint spatter effect.

65 Here, the flame design has been done as a simple pinstripe.

66 Dale Dinse's two-tone '34 Chevy is very elegant and combines a flame and a graphic design.

67 And a simple graphic design in back.

68 The break between the two colors uses a flame design in front.

Truck Flames

69 Here's something not seen too often: two wildly flamed big rigs, nose to nose. Two very different styles of flame paint, yet very similar in design.

70 There have been a number of trucks already seen in this chapter, but some trucks are more utility-like than others—trucks that normally aren't flamed like this heavy-duty truck.

71 Here's a 350 Super Duty with two layers of flames. The softly airbrushed white flame on gray flame on white base makes for a very cool monochromatic effect.

72 This two-layer flamed work van uses only one taped-off flame. The red flame is most likely taped-off basecoat red.

73 Airbrushed woodgrain with cool white flames faded with candy blue. Very wild. It sure spices up this old window wagon.

74 This is one wild old truck. It's come a long way from the 1930s when it was probably used for over-the-road hauling.

75 Bold and bright, this truck screams "look at me!" with these wild flames, a dark base with blue-tipped orange flames. Remember, orange and blue complement each other.

76 This classic fire truck carries its own fire with it.

77 While tribal flames are not common on classic trucks, on sport trucks they are right at home. These are classic hot rod colors with a tribal twist on this Ford Ranger.

78 While the flame shape may be familiar, the rest of this paint job is uniquely sport truck territory. A simple two-tone is broken up by a wild flame filled with hundreds of skull patterns.

79 Can the New Age Family Truckster be cool? Just add flames. It's probably the coolest car at soccer practice. Note how the flames start out as a reverse flame.

Pinstriped Flames

80 Pinstriped flames are not all that common on cars. But every once in a while, one can be found.

81 Here, the pinstriped flames are limited to the front fenders. Very unique.

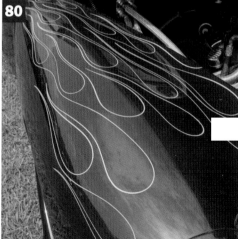

Small Details

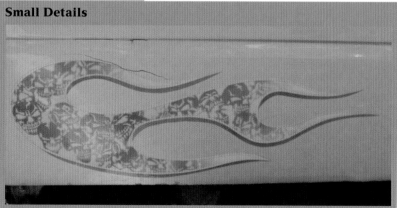

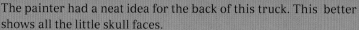

The painter had a neat idea for the back of this truck. This better shows all the little skull faces.

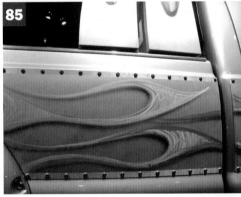

Metal Flames

82 Most likely the hardest part of this unpainted car's process was coating the body with copper. The flames were most likely taped off, and then a textured pad was wiped over the exposed surface, creating the dull sheen seen here.

83 This old Chevy wagon has some serious flames, all painted in candy tones over bare metal that has had a grinder run over it.

84 A close-up of the ground metal flames. Wicked cool.

85 On this truck the flames have actually been sketched out in the metal with a grinder. Notice the airbrushed shadows under the flames.

Realistic Flames

86 Realistic fire flames are painted by many airbrush artists, and each one has a unique way of painting them. The trick is to achieve a looseness in the flames so they look natural and not structured. This is my version of real flames as seen on the hood of a '39 Ford.

87 Another painter's vision of real fire flames. It is looser than mine but still has a very real, if not more real, look to it.

88 Here, the flames are limited to the front fenders. The colors are more subtle with no yellow. Just reds and oranges.

89 These real flames are very different from the other examples, yet they look real. There is no one way to paint these flames.

90 One cool thing about real flames is that images can be airbrushed into the flames. Here, a few skull faces peer out.

91 These real fire flames have lots of movement and all kinds of ghostly faces peeking out from the flames.

92 Here, the flames form into a cobra under the hood scoop.

93 Dean McCluster's '34 Ford was flamed by Chris Ellis, who layered traditional flames in black over a layer of real flames.

94 Raymond Mays wanted real flames on his '32 Ford, but he wanted them to be very subtle. I kept most of the yellow at the very front of the car. I used very thinned-down colors for the flames so they would have a very translucent effect.

95 Traditional-style flames layered over subtle real fire flames.

Graphics on
Motorcycles

L ook over the photos in this chapter and try to imagine how the various ideas would look using different colors or different techniques. What if a line was changed here or there? One of the ways to come up with new ideas is to be inspired by a technique you see in one place, a color seen somewhere else, and a design that could be redrawn to be more in tune to your project. Many artists pick up ideas from everywhere, taking bits and pieces and restructuring them into a brand-new idea.

1 A graphic paint job is anything that is not flame-shaped or involves mural or photographic-style artwork. Graphic paint can be as simple as the paint on this Redneck Eng. chopper: green basecoat with very simple purple and red graphic designs.

2 Or graphic paint can be as wild and complex as it can get. Joe Pro's custom-built Perewitz custom. Paint by Keith Hanson.

Simple Graphic Paint
Killer custom graphics don't have to be extreme or involve countless hours. Take a look at these tanks and paint jobs and see for yourself.

3 A simple, sleek stripe down the center of a custom tank is perfect on this custom bike by Bill Steele.

4 Basic rally stripe down the center of this peanut tank. Note the shadow under the stripes. An uncomplicated design with strong impact.

5 A silver streak and airbrushed stars race down the center of the stretched tank on this Donnie Smith custom. A classic, timeless design.

6 When I painted this tank I used a metal-effect technique to make it complement the top profile of the tank.

7 Here's a long, narrow tank using a similar metal-effect technique. The design emphasizes the length of the tank.

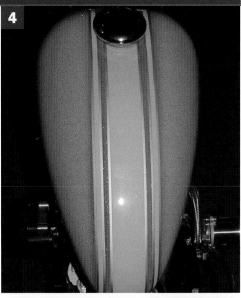

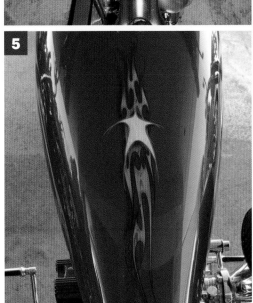

Unique Pinstripes

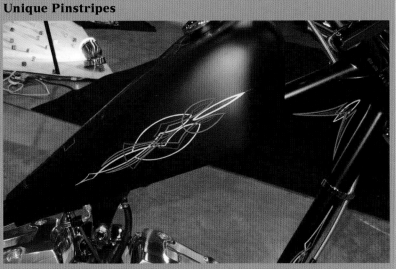

Not the average pinstripe layout. Not a traditional location for this kind of narrow layout. Check out the striping on the frame. Custom paint is all about the unusual.

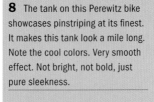

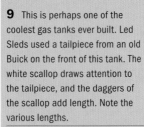

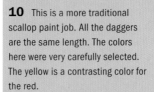

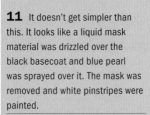

8 The tank on this Perewitz bike showcases pinstriping at its finest. It makes this tank look a mile long. Note the cool colors. Very smooth effect. Not bright, not bold, just pure sleekness.

9 This is perhaps one of the coolest gas tanks ever built. Led Sleds used a tailpiece from an old Buick on the front of this tank. The white scallop draws attention to the tailpiece, and the daggers of the scallop add length. Note the various lengths.

10 This is a more traditional scallop paint job. All the daggers are the same length. The colors here were very carefully selected. The yellow is a contrasting color for the red.

11 It doesn't get simpler than this. It looks like a liquid mask material was drizzled over the black basecoat and blue pearl was sprayed over it. The mask was removed and white pinstripes were painted.

12 Here's a close-up of the V-Rod seen in Chapter 6. Since it's a color-changing basecoat that changes from purple to red to cinnamon to gold, it requires artwork in a color that will go with all those colors. I picked tones of black and white, airbrushing a metal effect.

Graphics on Stock Paint

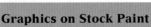

This is a stock Harley-Davidson paint job—with a twist. Look at the sides of the rear fender and the top of the tank. On a factory job those areas do not have artwork. Some clever painter added those extra panels and the red slashes with gold zigzags right on top of the stock paint. Stock factory paint with a simple metal-effect tribal flame graphic added.

13 Several unusual factors are present in this basic two-tone paint job. The color combination is not common, yet they are nearly contrasting colors. And notice the very trick graphic border separating the colors. Look closely at the blue. See the patterns? Many good ideas here.

14 Another two-tone, and another unique way of separating the colors, this time by bringing the red into the white as a tribal design. Note the subtle yellow shading just under the red, adding a glow and softening the transition between the red and white.

15 More great ideas come together. A metal-effect border at the front, a bright blue panel that ends in an interesting jagged edge, plus two pink streamers that add movement. Many different surfaces working together.

16 A very fascinating yet simple graphic effect seen here. The area was taped off, a screen was placed over the surface, and black was sprayed.

17 Similar colors, a simple liquid tribal graphic, but heavy impact. Why? It's the interesting way the design plays across the surface.

18 A very slick liquid graphic effect over a rainbow pearl surface. The design was taped off and black was airbrushed around the edges. Then white highlights were added, making the graphic look like drops of water, even water that looks to be in the shape of an eagle.

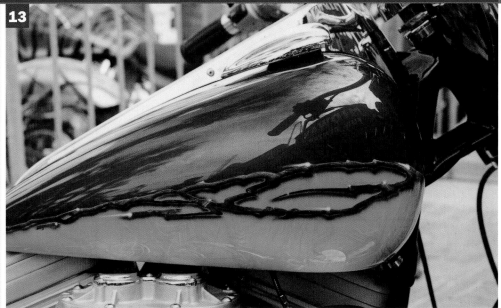

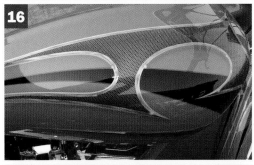

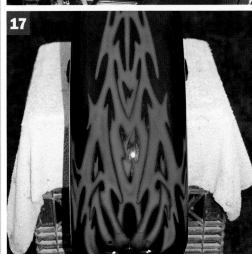

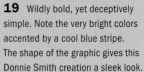

19

20

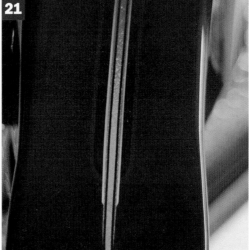

21

19 Wildly bold, yet deceptively simple. Note the very bright colors accented by a cool blue stripe. The shape of the graphic gives this Donnie Smith creation a sleek look.

20 Here's an example of how to get a great idea. It's a simple design, but see the trick? The basecoat of this paint job is silver foil leaf. The design was done over the leaf. This way the design casts a shadow over the leaf, creating real depth. Use a silver leaf basecoat, but put a different graphic over it. Maybe apply a few coats of candy first.

21 Making a big impact with very little line. This sweet little striped design accents the top of a rear fender. Just enough to break up the red base.

Multilayered Graphics

22 There are many good ideas happening on the front fender of this Leroy Thompson bike: the spatter coat center stripe, the floating stars over the surface, and more. There are many layers, but they are quite simple if you break them down. Note the monochromatic tones.

22

Small Accents

Little details make all the difference. This Paul Yaffe creation does not have much artwork. Highly detailed, very slender, graphic silver foil leaf designs accent corners and body lines.

Design problem: What kind of graphic design will fit on this fender? The fender has "scales," and the design must work with them.
Solution: Add silver foil leaf stars that accent the rear point of the fender and scales.

23 Looks simple, but it is not. This is a study in subtle tones. A very soft shading of dark yellows creates the lower layer of graphics. Then the blue layer is added and shadowed. Keeping the tones even is hard when working with such subtle colors.

24 This native design is very trick, stretching from the tank onto the frame, lengthening the tank. Warm, earthy tones work well with the design.

25 Another monochromatic paint job, this time using layers of silver and charcoal tones with multiple layers of more stone effect. The shadowing brings it to life.

26 Closely related, mostly noncontrasting colors, beautiful design fades. A very small amount of one contrasting color. All combine to give this paint job endless depth and interest.

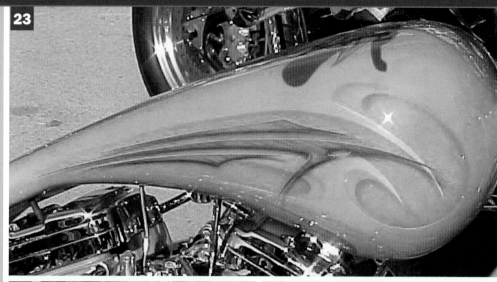

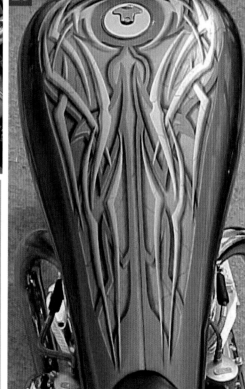

Rear Fender Issues

One big problem can be how to handle a rear fender design that works with the taillight and plate area. Here, Keith Hanson handled it in a very straightforward way: He simply went over it.

27 Keith Hanson is a master of multilayered graphics, which can be very tedious to do. Look closely at these next few jobs and know that each different color is a separate tape-out or carefully laid pinstripe.

28 Dave Perewitz and Keith get crazy on this bike. Contrasting and complementary colors, striped, spattered, and airbrushed. Note the subtle base color. Would it be as effective if the basecoat had been a bright color?

29 Another extreme paint job from Dave and Keith, but with a bold base color. Very similar to the last one with airbrushed and spattered tones with solid color and gold leaf striping. This is the result of many years' experience of working with color and design.

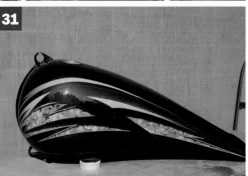

30 I had to combine a graphic and a logo for this charity bike. Note the colors and checkered effect on the logo. I worked them into the graphic.

31 Here's a multilayered paint job I did a few years ago. I used a granite effect for one of the layers.

32 This is a slender bike. The graphics emphasize this by being very sleek and lean. Lots of points and thin lines, and a very small amount of bright color.

33 This multilayered paint job proves why Chris Cruz is one of the finest custom painters in the world. The bottom layer is a rusty metal effect, complete with bullet hole. A tattered flag is another layer. Even the purple layer is airbrushed to look like the basecoat black is turning into purple fabric.

34 Here's a bold pearl orange basecoat with similar and contrasting color graphics and a cool carbon fiber effect for the lowest layer of graphics.

35 Plaid on a bike? Darren from Liquid Illusions Custom Paint came up with this incredible plaid paint for Stevenson's Cycle Build-Off bike. Note the one solid stripe that breaks up the plaid. This paint is a study in colors and design working together in complete harmony.

When Old Is New Again

36 French Kiss paints some of the coolest retro-styled paint on the planet. They are bringing back the very best custom paint elements from the 1960s and 1970s. Here, they used scaling on the sides and lace panels on the top of this Sucker Punch Sally custom.

37 Another Sucker Punch Sally bike with another French Kiss paint job. Rainbow flake basecoat is layered with candy green and yellow. Thinned-down black sprayed through a stencil creates a random pattern. One trick for custom painters is to have a design on the top that is not an exact duplicate of the design on the sides, yet it's compatible with the side design. French Kiss solves that problem very neatly.

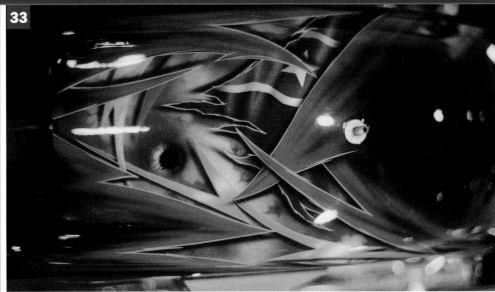

Special Effects

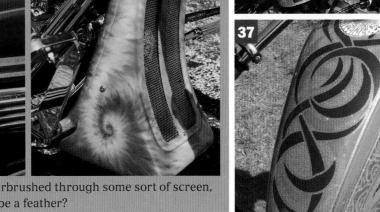

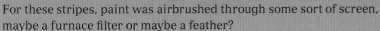

For these stripes, paint was airbrushed through some sort of screen, maybe a furnace filter or maybe a feather?

This is one wildly and cleverly airbrushed spoiler. The tie-dye effect is very real. This would be a great effect to fill a graphic design.

38 French Kiss paint on a Bling's Cycle. Subtle shading and panels make a big impact.

39 Carefully examine this rear fender. Look at the different panel designs and the various graphic effects used for them.

40 Oil tank on a Leroy Thompson custom with designs influenced by 1960s paint. Incredible creativity at work. A killer lace seam separates the panels.

41 My customer wanted something simple yet striking and retro to go on his Yamaha bobber. I went with a red flake basecoat and simple panel art. I designed retro panels with a modern twist.

Oil Tank Designs

Chris Cruz produces some of the best-designed paint in the world. His way of working the oil tank into the design is nothing short of amazing. But this same way of continuing a tank design can be used to design artwork for fenders, saddlebags, farings—anywhere on the bike.

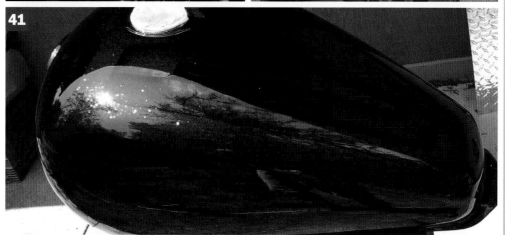

This native-styled border wraps around the oil tank. The design is quite simple but ingenious.

Look closely at the different artwork techniques on this tank and try to figure out how they were done.

Graphic Ideas
for Baggers

42 Who says baggers are not custom bikes? The days of boring baggers are over. More and more people are customizing their full dresser bikes, like this street glide. The graphic starts at the headlight, stretches across the tank, sidecovers, and onto the bags.

43 Dave Perewitz and Keith Hanson did an incredible job on this bagger. Note the soft colors for the graphic. Easy on the eyes.

44 A Donnie Smith bagger. Sleek design and soft colors. Smooth.

45 This bagger from Tex EFX is a thing of beauty. Tex McDorman and his son Critte put a lot of hours into this bike. Underneath the red candy are tons of detailed airbrush work.

46 Here's how Paul Yaffe does a bagger. One thing it has in common with the previous baggers is the limited color selection. It gives a normally fat bike a sleek look.

47 My version of a custom bagger. Keeping the design sleek and colors subtle.

48 Not sure what to call this effect. But the color selection is perfect and the design flows nicely with the lines of the bike.

Faring Effects

49 Factory paint with simple pinstriping. Many times adding artwork to stock paint can really change the appearance.

50 Simple and very effective multilayer graphics fit beautifully on this faring.

51 Layers of metal-effect tribal flames work with the lines of this faring.

52 Pretty wild, but a neat paint idea. A graphic skull peeks out from graphic slashes.

53 Compare the faring design and the front fender design. Very harmonious.

54 And here's a different way of painting a faring. This time the design is limited to the top surface.

Saddlebag Solutions

55 This is a sweet mixture of tribal graphics and mural artwork. As these bags have crash guards, the design must be high on the bags. Paint by Chris Cruz.

56 This clever native-style design actually works the baglights into the design. Art by Chris Cruz.

57 One of the first baggers I painted. Lots of design, but subtle, cool colors keep it sleek.

58 Elegant gray pinstriping is all this Yaffe bagger needs.

59 Yet a different way of ending a bagger design: bringing both sides of the design together on the rear fender.

60 Very effective and wild design on these bags. Again, note the subtle colors.

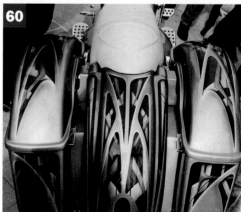

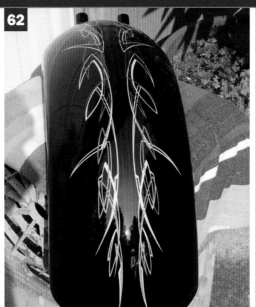

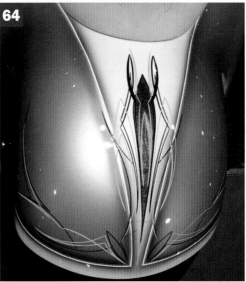

And Then There's Pinstriping

61 Evil sweet striping on the rear fender of a Bling's Cycle.

62 Ryan Young striped this fender for an *American Iron* magazine project bike. Look carefully at the thickness of the stripes and the colors used: cream white, copper, and burgundy. All deep, warm colors.

63 Pinstriping on candy-coated ground metal. Sweet.

64 These are some very trick graphics: soft shading on the paneled colors, silver leaf shaded with candy blue, framed by graceful pinstriping.

Behind the 8 ball

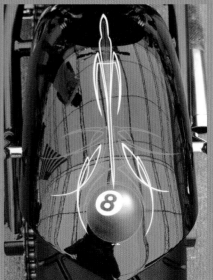

Two different bikes, one cool idea: mixing mural work with pinstriping.

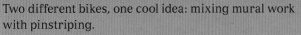
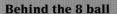

65 This pinstriping is so simple and pure. The rounded end of the white is cool and neat.

66 Close-up of the pinstriped art on the previous bike. Soft colors, yet high impact.

67 The graphic design on this already long bike sleeks it out and makes it appear even longer. Black and white and a little striping bring it together.

Lettering as an Art

68 I came up with this great graphic many years ago. Simple, yet it needed something more. An airbrushed emblem is perfect.

69 Chrome-effect lettering by Bill Streeter, perfectly mixing mural work and graphics.

70 Close-up of some very radical chrome lettering. The "D" is actually a dragon.

71 Beautifully thought-out shading on this lettering. It looks like metal, but it's not airbrushed the way metal is normally done.

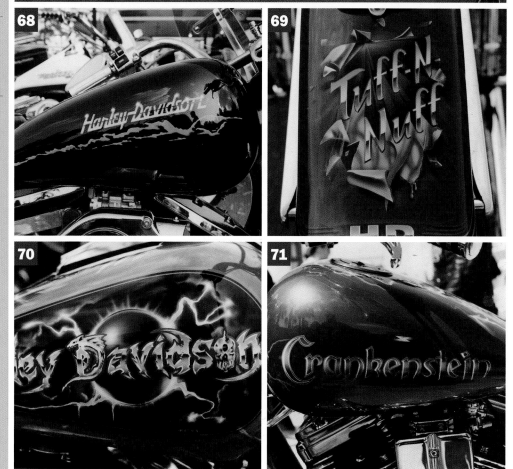

72

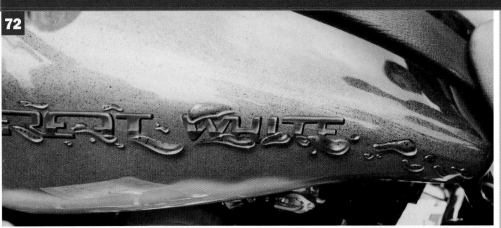

73

74

75

76

77

78

72 Chrome-effect letters with water trailing from them. Note the way the surface under the water drops is magnified. Very clever.

73 A simple and very effective metal effect lettering by Bill Streeter.

74 Upsweep lettering by Liquid Illusions done with variegated gold leaf. Perfectly complements the tank's shape.

75 An extremely cool idea on this Bling's Cycle.

76 A very unique tank on this Chica custom with some beautifully graceful lettering.

Is It Airbrushed Murals or Graphics?

77 This is a really cool effect. Stone-effect airbrushed behind the graphic with a skull face forming out of the stone.

78 Incredibly airbrushed tiki-themed bike. Orange base with candy tangerine shading around Hawaiian designs. The silver design down the center balances the layout.

79 Tribal graphic with wild skull coming from behind it. Very cool.

80 Skulls have flames coming off them, so why not graphics?

81 Using similar colors and an effective design, this tribal lengthens the tank. Maybe this kind of design would be perfect for framing a mural?

82 Killer technique used here to create a stone-effect marble surface.

83 Stone-effect granite is a great material to use for graphics.

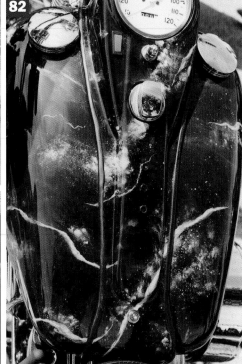

Chris Cruz Graphics

Chris Cruz and his amazing sense of design. He comes up with the perfect graphics to come off the gas cap area of bike tanks.

1 What are graphics? Are they two-toning a car? Or pinstripes? Or something more complex? They are all of that and more. They are just about anything that is not definite flame or mural artwork. Like seen here. A two-tone paint job gone extreme. Extreme complementary colors. Orange on the long lower section of the car emphasizes it. A few evil jags. But the orange brings out the best aspects of this work of rolling art.

Four-Wheeled Works of
Graphic Art

What are graphics? Are they two-toning a car? Or pinstripes? Or something more complex? They are all of that and more. They are just about anything that is not definite flame or mural artwork. The wonderful thing about a graphic paint scheme is that it can be unique. New and interesting designs can be dreamed up. Take a close look at the some of the examples seen in this chapter. Some design ideas focus on bold lines. Others use shadowy detail to achieve an effect. And yet others combine the two. The great thing about graphics is that a design can be changed simply by moving a few lines or adding a few lines.

Two-Tone Graphics

2 Most cars split the two tones along the upper body line, such as this low rider. But it is not a simple two-tone. Sly graphic effects run along the division of colors. Examine the unique sponge shadowing under the main color break. The airbrushed chrome-effect stripe ends at a neat little airbrushed checkered flag emblem and the pink and green zag.

3 Another body line rule breaker. But it makes use of the rear wheelwell. Note the airbrushed chrome stripe. Very clean design.

4 Breaking on the body line with a very simple graphic on this Willys. Black and green are a very powerful combination.

5 Very quiet yet powerful two-tone. Look closely at the design between the colors. Very slick metal-effect emblem design.

6 Classic two-tone on this Ford truck. Neat graphic between the colors. Very simple.

7 Purple on purple two-tone. Cool color break.

8 Another uniquely designed color break. This time on an import tuner.

9 Very killer idea. No stripe along the color break, but rather a design just below it to set it off. The shading gives depth to the whole design of the paint.

10 Very detailed, multilayered color break design on this mini truck.

11 Close-up of the detailed artwork. Note the beveling on the chrome-effect graphic.

12 It looks like a simple two-tone Mustang from afar.

13 But the flames' color break design is very detailed. Beveled edge flames, pinstriping, careful shadowing, and little skull faces in the flames.

14 Is it a two-tone? Whatever it is, it's pretty cool. It's a combination of two-tone, scallops, and a checkered flag mural. Many great ideas working together here.

15 Another simple graphic design with a slick mood. Note the lettering along the striping. Very neat.

16 Very clean, quiet design on this sedan. It literally wraps around the car and ties it together.

17 A small design that speaks loudly by using color combinations and fine detail.

18 Nice two-tone with an engine-turned gold leaf design on the quarter panel. Imagine the car without the design. The design gives the car's paint a lot more pop.

19 Super sweet rock-effect design on the top quarter of this Chevy. The blue adds zip.

20 This is one very clever design. Lots of depth and impact with very little detail work. Notice the soft colors with the exception of the bright red pinstripe.

21 Wood-effect color break design that ends in a neat tribal pattern. It gives an elegant feel to this Camaro.

The Traditional Rear Quarter Design

I don't know if there is a term for it, but many painters find that the perfect place for a graphic is the front top edge of the rear quarter panel.

A Little Something for Single Colors

How do you give a single-color car a little something to make it stand out without getting overly involved in artwork? Sometimes a great basecoat color and a little accent graphic can make a big statement.

22 Close-up of the accent design in the next photo. This is actually a very trick design. See the white? It is actually three-dimensional. It can be felt, and as it is not flat on the surface, it casts a shadow.

23 Powder blue sedan, but a little bit of design breaks up the blue just enough to make it interesting.

24 Another subtle but cool design. It appears that it was made by using a sponge and pinstriping technique.

25 Completely incredible basecoat. Most likely a white base was applied, and then the orange was applied. Note the body line and the chrome strip. See how well the accent design works with these elements.

26 Close-up of the accent design. It's unreal how awesome this is. Note the classic Chevy insignia inside the chrome-effect design. Ghost images of that design appear in the purple stripe, almost like a diamond plate effect.

27 Another amazing orange car with a clever accent graphic.

28 The beautiful detail is only seen close up. Soft airbrushing of shadows and highlights combined with careful color selection. Note how pink was used on both orange cars.

29 There is no real rule for accent graphics. Evil black street rod, and the checkerboard firewall gives it even more punch.

30 Clever way to separate a two-tone. It was the only artwork on this car.

Pinstriping

31 Or striping can get very detailed. This tailgate design is by Ryan Young.

32 Pinstriping can make a very big impact. Another picture of this car is seen at the beginning of this chapter. Big surface but small, very effective design.

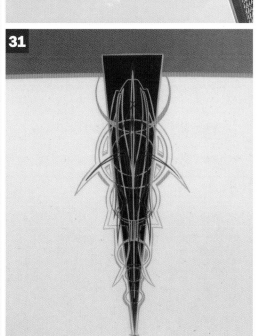

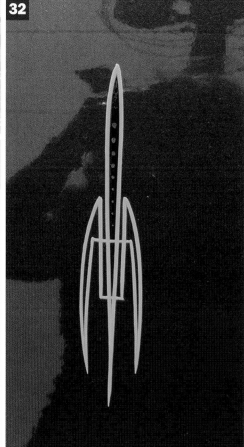

33

34

35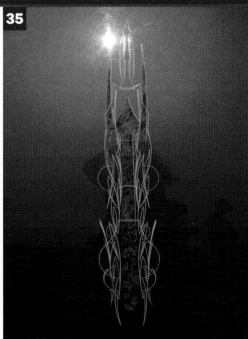

36

37

38

39

40

33 Or it can get very, very intricate.

34 Interesting design on the tailgate of this truck. Great use of color.

35 Note the color choices on this mix of cracked stone and striping: banana yellow with dark pink. But it works, and it looks great.

A Little Bit of Lettering

36 Now this is some tiny lettering. Smaller than a dime.

37 Classic turned gold leaf lettering.

38 & 39 Small details like this are what make for cool paint jobs. Instead of just lettering over the stripe, the artist airbrushed a rip and put the lettering in that.

40 "Stuff"? I love the purple granite-effect triangle.

Scallops

41 One of the oldest graphic styles is the scallop. Here's a sedan with a classic-style scallop. Note the blue bottom edges, which add dimension.

42 What is different about these scallops? At first glance they look standard. Look at where the scallops start. See the pattern? The green tips make a big difference in the way the purple and yellow work together.

43 A very traditional scallop design. The white front end makes the front of the car look bigger. It doesn't show in this photo, but there is a purple pearl flip-flop overlay on the white. When the sun hits it right, the purple glows.

44 A reverse scallop? Why not?

45 Only from the mind of the Canadian Rat Fink. Charcoal pearl front end accented with a blue fade edge. Wow.

Rare Custom Paint

It is rare to see radical graphic custom paint on classic cars. Most people flame them. This is why there is only one photo of muscle car graphic paint in this book. If you have a muscle car and want wild paint, check out 1960s and '70s car magazines. Look for wild old-style paint. Look through Chapter 10 at the retro style bike paint to see what I mean. Think outside the box by looking back.

Getting Radical with Graphics

46 Radical tuner and sport cars deserve to have radical paint. Simple two-tone? Not quite. A simple zag makes it edgy.

47 Little red sports car. A graceful yet evil black tribal cuts across it. Note the silver striping on the tribal.

48 Normally I wouldn't put red and blue together, but this painter used white pearl as a base and it all comes together nice, cool, and edgy.

49 Again, a wild design with limited colors. Green and blue are contrasting colors. Note that the hood is off the car. The design goes from the grille area into the engine compartment and out to the windshield.

50 The hood better shows the true colors. Look closely at the sides of the hood. There are skulls in the smoke.

51 Nice mixture of flames and graphics happening on this hood. Another example of limited color selection working effectively with the design.

New Ideas

Is it a flame or graphic? This unusual flame paint has a layout that is more like graphics. This is why custom sport vehicles are a great source of cutting-edge ideas.

52 This is really cool paint. Wonderful color fade from front to back with airbrushed texture that helps the fade. The rusty diamond plate effect works effectively with the warm tones of the orange. Airbrushed mural can be a great layer under graphics.

53 A close-up of the next paint job. Now the extreme detail can easily be seen: super-fine green striping, airbrushed fading, shadow skulls, and even the shadow of a logo.

54 It may be a drag car, but this is a great paint idea for any vehicle.

Big Ideas from Mini Trucks

55 Looking for radical paint ideas? Look no further than a mini truck. Examine this paint and note all the different effects. The way the colors all work together. Even the bed of this pickup is very detailed.

56 A simple tribal design down the sides of this mini truck.

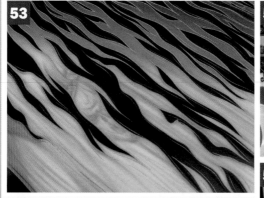

Work With It

Keep an open mind! Just because you don't like the color of a vehicle, it doesn't mean it can't give you great ideas. The colors on this mini truck are very subtle. But let's say you like bright colors and don't look closely at the truck. Then you are missing out on a great idea for a color break design. The downward spikes could angle and stagger differently. Take an idea, be inspired, redesign, and make it your own.

57 Now take a similar design and add a layer of airbrushed artwork underneath it. Always think of ways to improve or add to a design or idea.

58 Very extreme graphic artwork here. It was all done freehand with an airbrush or small paint gun. Great idea that leads to other ideas. What if some of the layers had been taped off then sprayed? What if some of the lines were changed?

59 Here's the tailgate of this truck. While the whole tailgate is pretty cool, the fuzzy, just-out-of-focus checkered pattern at the lower right is incredible. The white and black flow and dissipate into the purple.

60 Another graphic full of possibilities. Here's a great idea on a cool truck, but instead of copying this idea, redesign it. Change the spikes. Make them longer. Instead of a solid color on the bottom, fill that area with an airbrushed graphic effect.

61 Very unique design layout on the hood. Liquid graphic down the side while the two lower layers form a circle.

62 Similar color basecoat and graphics stretch across this ride. Look closely, as there are actually two layers of graphics here. Very sleek. But there's more.

63 The top graphic goes straight across the top center of the truck. Subtle, earthy colors and wood effect go great with the white base.

64 Another hood design. Airbrushed with orange candy fades, tribal flames on the right of the hood. A jagged purple graphic rips across the width and continues down onto and across the sides of the body. The purple also has airbrushing.

65 The left side of the truck. Very cool and full of ideas for more paint schemes.

66 The hardtop cover of the bed. Note how the side graphic comes up and is part of the cover. Very unusual basecoat color—peach. But it works great with the graphics.

67 Many times painters bring the graphics up the hood and across the top of the truck, keeping the design on one side or the other. Look at all the things going on in this "simple" graphic strip.

68 Ron Gibbs filled these graphics with many different effects: marbleizing airbrushed smoke, tribal patterns, and fades. It has so much depth and boldness.

Four-Wheeled Works of **Graphic Art**

69 Bad photo of a great mini truck paint job. It's a very effective overall design. Clever tiki graphics, and the white, black, and orange work great together.

70 Now examine the detailed paint in the truck's bed. Close up, the fine detail airbrushing in the white and orange can be seen.

71 More wild colors slashing wildly across this SUV.

72 Wild colors contrasting and complementing each other. Very bold and bright.

73 Another wild color selection. Green and brown? It sure works great here. It helps that there is so much tone variation in the airbrushed murals in the brown layer.

74 Flames or graphics? This time it's both. Paint by Razor Custom Paint Shop.

Custom Truck Paint

75 Pickup trucks have always been cool, but with custom paint they can look even cooler. Speaking of cool, blue and purple contrast each other beautifully on this Dodge.

76 A wicked, wild graphic filled with lightning. Blue and white are so strong together. But what makes it pop is the hard-edged shadow beneath the lightning.

77 Note the way the graphic goes under the windshield onto the dash. You can also see the detail work in this Ron Gibbs graphic.

78 Ron Gibbs did an amazing job on this Dodge. Complementary colors paired with silver and metal effect.

79 Why have a black Hummer just like everyone else? Look closely and find the ghost images in this paint. Note the shadowing. But the green pinstriping really wakes it up.

Small Details

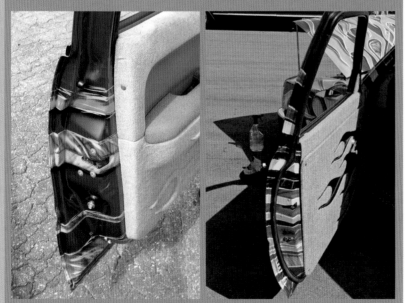

Don't forget the door jambs. Killer custom paint goes around edges and into places that are sometimes ignored. But that little detail makes a big difference.

Murals on
Motorcycles

1 Just a pair of feathers with an airbrushed, beaded, native-style border. Sometimes a mural doesn't have to be complex to make its point.

2 Here, the background becomes the foreground. The forest in back rolls out past the fawn to become a major feature of the mural. Art by Chris Cruz.

Murals can range from simple to very complex. It's all in the design. Most of the time, the customer works with the artist to bring a vision to life. Are there any particular rules for murals? Not really. The best rule of thumb is to keep it simple and to remember the color wheel. Use it to guide you. The more complex a mural is, the more careful the color design needs to be.

3 Mural or graphic? Here, a smoky lightning-style mist plays behind a tribal graphic. Note the way the artwork gracefully dances across the whole surface of this Tour-Pak. Simple and beautiful.

4 For the most part, a mural is an airbrushed background with a character in the foreground. Here, we have a grassy plain at sunset with a horse.

5 Another sunset scene, this time with wolves. Notice how the wolves are in black silhouette with just a hint of light around them. It appears more complex than it actually is. Paint by Chris Cruz.

6 These clouds sweep around the whole tank and are not limited to only one surface of the tank. There are no hard rules for mural design.

7 Background: desert and clouds. Foreground: eagle flying. The emphasis is on the fine detail, the clouds, the rock formations, and the eagle.

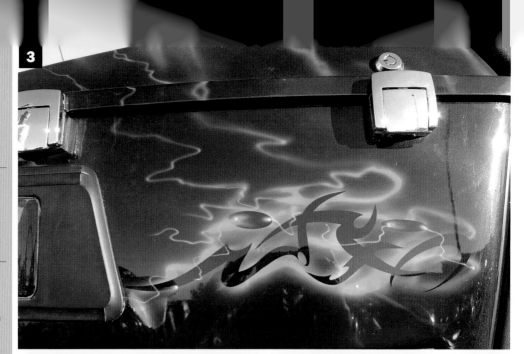

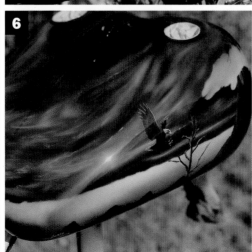

8

9

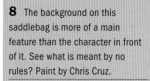

10

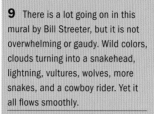

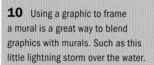

11

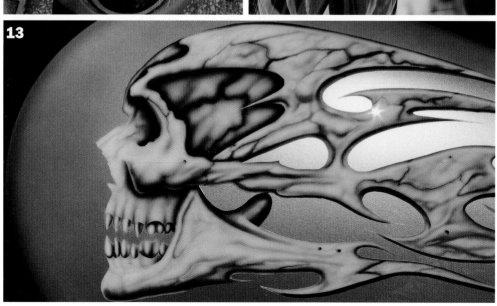

12

13

8 The background on this saddlebag is more of a main feature than the character in front of it. See what is meant by no rules? Paint by Chris Cruz.

9 There is a lot going on in this mural by Bill Streeter, but it is not overwhelming or gaudy. Wild colors, clouds turning into a snakehead, lightning, vultures, wolves, more snakes, and a cowboy rider. Yet it all flows smoothly.

10 Using a graphic to frame a mural is a great way to blend graphics with murals. Such as this little lightning storm over the water.

11 Look closely at this mural framed with graphics. There's quite a bit going on in it, but the limited use of color keeps it from going overboard.

Skull Paint

12 One of the most common things to paint on motorcycles is skulls. Here I turned the back of a skull into tribal flames, using the bone effect for the flame surface.

13 This is the area just below the neck on a bike frame. Note how the graphics have been airbrushed to come together as a skull face.

14 Fitto is a master of painting skulls. This little skull is less than two inches across. Another blend of murals and graphics.

15 Just a simple mural of a lightning storm? Look again—notice the skull face coming out of the clouds?

16 Here, Mike Learn combines graphics and murals with a skull peeking out of a graphic.

17 One of the most popular skulls I have ever painted. The backward-capped skull. What makes it striking is the color combination. Mostly purples with a hint of blue. Purple and blue are similar yet different tones of contrasting colors.

18 Mike Learn is a master of painting skulls. Here, he uses soft, similar tones in a very complex mural of many skulls.

19 Vince Goodeve is another amazing artist. Here, he uses similar colors in a tattoo-like effect for a very complex skull mural on a Rick Fairless custom chopper.

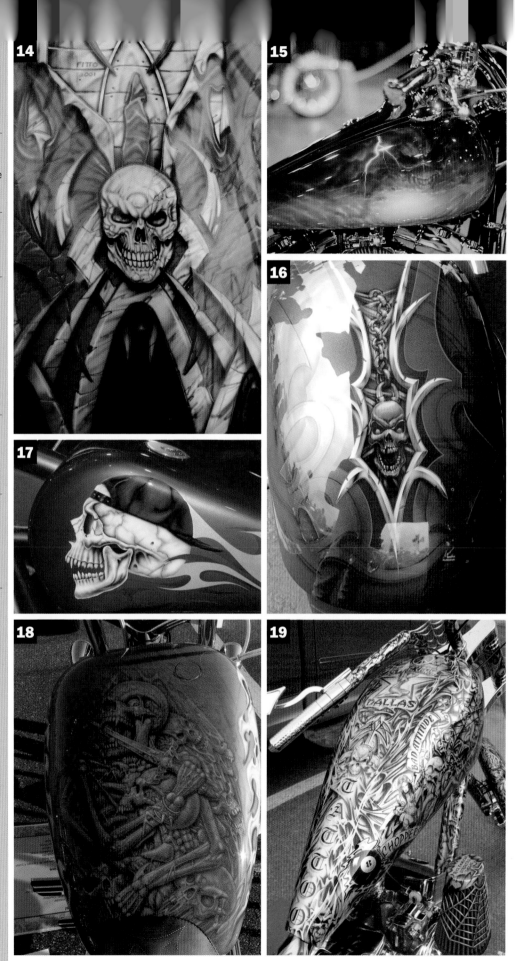

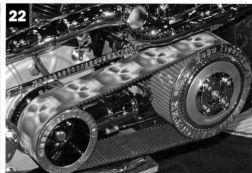

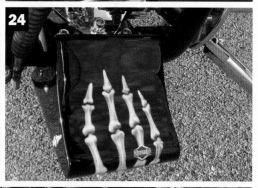

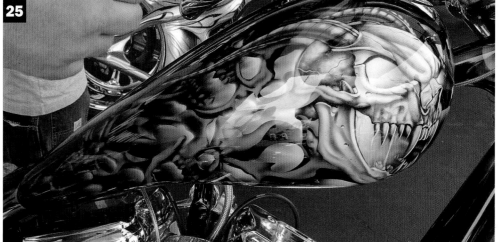

20 But skulls don't have to be complex to be striking. Here, a tribal graphic filled with skull faces makes a big impact.

21 I used a simple tribal design and filled it with skulls in similar colors.

22 Sometimes the coolest murals are not on the sheet metal of the bike. Here, ghostly repetitive skulls grace the primary belt.

23 This artist combined skulls and a mechanical background.

24 Another simple idea with heavy impact: a skeleton hand coming up from under an airdam.

25 This masterpiece by Bill Streeter is an amazing example of images using darks and lights to achieve depth and form. The very subtle background shading creates a solid web of skull faces.

26 The first good eagle mural I painted back in the 1980s. The eagle flying out of the darkness. Not much wing detail. The emphasis is on the head and feet, yet there is a lot of depth to this mural.

27 Natural background, eagle flying. Note how the positioning of the wings fits neatly to the shape of the tank.

28 The shape of this eagle seems to be a perfect fit for this fairing. Art by Robert Gorski.

29 Eagles can be airbrushed in many different styles. Here, Chris Cruz uses a very realistic approach. The color selection for the background is incredible.

30 Bill Streeter uses a more stylized technique for this eagle mural. Notice how effective the soft shading is.

31 Dawne Holmes goes all the way with a stylized approach in this eagle mural. Look at the amazing use of subtle shading to achieve the metal look of the eagle.

Eagles

As popular as skulls, maybe even more so, eagles and motorcycles seem to go together. But how do you make your eagle paint stand out from all the others? Check out the following examples and come up with your own unique eagle mural.

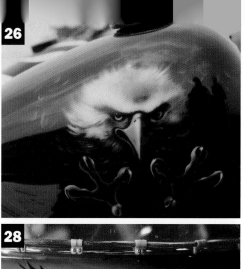

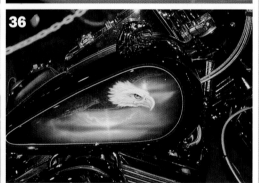

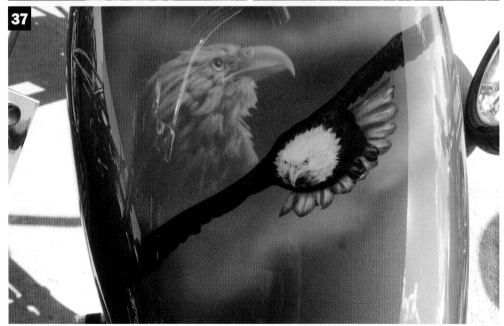

32 Here, Sonny DePalma combines metal and feathers for a semirobotic eagle.

33 And on this bike, Sonny goes all the way. A mechanical eagle head. The design work on this mural is nothing short of astounding.

34 Yet, compare that eagle to this extremely simple, stylized eagle by Dawne Holmes. Both have incredible design but are so very different.

35 The bigger the surface, the more detail is possible. For example, on this skirted fender, note the unusual way the light hits the eagle, making it dark.

36 The unusual thing about this beautiful mural is that it was done over a stock paint job, limited to the pinstriped paneled area. Very simple, yet full of depth. Art by Chris Cruz.

37 Two eagle murals in one. No detailed background, just an impression of blue sky, an eagle flying out of it, and the spirit of the eagle in the background. Very poignant.

38 Here, Chris Cruz takes the spirit of the eagle even further, combining an incredible cloud scene with an eagle head. Note how the cloud design and the positioning of the eagle effectively fit the shape of the fender.

39 Small details count. A ghost of a feather, with its shadow. Art by Sonny DePalma.

Flag Art

40 This fairing mural combines a flag background with an eagle foreground. Note how the stars have been airbrushed to look like stitches. Art by Mickey Harris.

41 Here's a great idea for a stock-style paint job. It keeps the flag art inside the paneled area.

42 A gracefully curled flag graces the side of this Dave Perewitz custom bike, accenting the shape of the tank.

43 The movement and depth airbrushed into this flag is incredible. Notice the rippled folds and the soft shading.

44 This is a very common idea that can be completely unique and individualized. Here, it's crossed flags and rifles against a shield. Sometimes artists use crossed swords or other weapons. The choices are limitless.

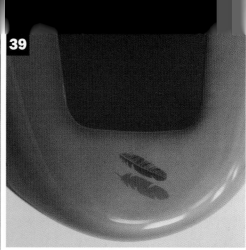

45

46

47

48

49

50

51

52

Native Themes

45 Native chiefs are very dramatic-looking and fit beautifully on the side of a motorcycle gas tank.

46 Here is a less stylized chief. Artist Chris Cruz has mastered the art of painting Native Americans. Note how perfectly the mural fits the shape of the tank.

47 Another chief mural from Chris Cruz. Look for the buffalo hidden in the headdress.

48 Another mural from Chris. The basecoat has been "torn away" and marbleizer has been applied. A ghost wolf leaps across the surface. The marbleizer makes the ghost image less noticeable.

49 Here's a few fender treatments from Chris Cruz. Many people feel that there is no room for a mural on the rear fender of a stock bike, but a warrior face fits quite neatly under this taillight.

50 A front fender mural from the same bike. The warrior's horse fits beautifully on the top of this fender.

51 There are so many cool ideas going on here, I don't know where to start: the amazing graphic design, the filler technique for the graphic, the square shield, the feathers. This is a perfect example of thinking outside the box. Art by Chris Cruz.

52 This painted-on beaded bracelet is a neat little idea.

Animals

53 One of the most popular animals you will see on bikes is wolves. A snarling wolf face by Chris Cruz is perfectly suited for the top of this front fender and fits great between the graphic lines on the sides of the fender.

54 Another amazing piece of nature art from Chris. White wolf goes perfectly on a white bike.

55 Look closely at this wolf's eyes. See the ghost image? Art by Chris Cruz.

56 Here's a wolf I painted many years ago. It has a dreamy, mystical feel to it and goes perfectly on the candy blue basecoat.

57 How about a white tiger? The basecoat is a white tiger fur effect.

58 Frogs in the jungle? Why not?

59 Chris Cruz strikes again, this time with an underwater scene of whales, mermaids, sharks, and even a P40.

53

54

55

56

57

58

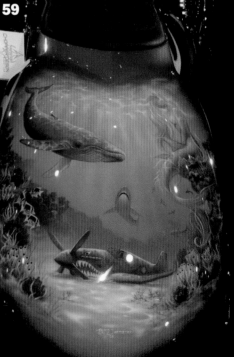

59

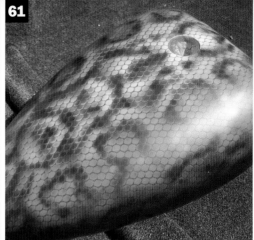

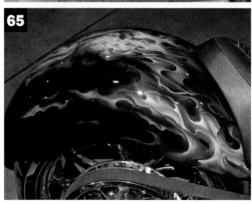

60 I painted some kind of creature here. I don't know what it is, but that's the beauty of mural work. Airbrushing fantasy.

Surface Textures

61 This snakeskin effect was achieved by first airbrushing the basecoat green, then stretching a net across the tank, then spraying the color tones. Paint by Ron Gibbs.

62 Granite is a fun surface to play with because various things can be "carved" in the granite. Here, the granite texture is blended with a ripped graphic.

63 Here, artist Chris Cruz has covered the surface with a stone effect and has done the graphic in a different colored stone.

64 Here, a liquid webbed surface serves as a background for a bone-effect cross.

65 Real fire flames were covered in previous chapters, but this is more like a real fire surface, not flames.

66 A metal-effect surface is paired with a bone or tendon effect. Note the seams and rusty spots. A silver basecoat was applied, and then black, white, and brown were softly airbrushed.

67 I don't know what this effect is supposed to be, but it sure is cool.

68 Another "don't know what it is," but it's way cool. Pretty awesome for just a black and white mural.

Pin-Up Girls

69 The classic pin-up girl.

70 Another classic pin-up, this one by Dawne Holmes. Bike by Keith Ball.

71 A very original pin-up girl by Keith Hanson.

72 Eddie Meeks painted the pin-up on the tank of this Cyril Huze creation.

73 An unusual design layout that works great. The artist, Sonny DePalma, puts the viewer into the mural, as if you are holding the cards and this is what you see.

1

2

Murals on
Four Wheels

Murals can range from small detail paintings to elaborate artwork that completely covers a vehicle. Whatever the size and style of a mural, it should complement the vehicle, not overpower it. Murals can also be used in combination with graphics and flames.

1 One of the most common places for mural artwork is on the tailgate of a truck. This tailgate mural by Bill Streeter is a classic: a woman on a horse running on the beach. Note the way the waves were airbrushed, and the colors that were used. Not the colors one would expect for a beach scene.

2 Here's a small detail mural done on a glovebox or airbag cover of a Ford truck. The mural features the truck itself. Art by Ron Gibbs.

3 A cute little tailgate mural featuring a cartoon character of a dragon, which is most likely the mascot of this truck.

4 Just a small detail, but it packs punch. A simple airbrushed Ford emblem.

5 Diamond plate is a great airbrushed effect. It can be used to fill up graphic areas, and it is rather easy to do.

6 Ghostly rows of skulls across the back of a Mustang trunk lid. Art by Ron Gibbs.

Chrome Effects

This chrome-effect lettering is airbrushed with white, blue, and black tones to achieve the chrome look.

On a different area of the car, the true effect of the airbrushing can be seen. A very skillfully airbrushed effect, it looks like a real chrome and engine-turned trim piece.

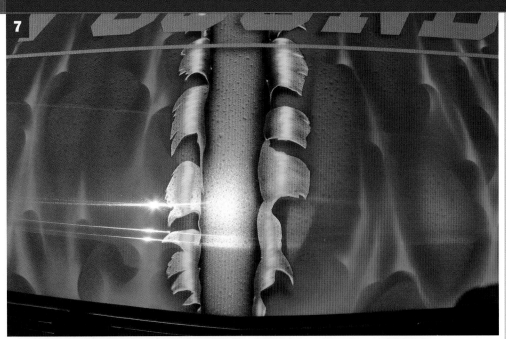

7 There are a number of different effects going on in this mural artwork. Ghostly real flame effects in green and blue, water drop effects in the middle silver strip, and peeled-back metal.

8 Not sure what to call the artwork effect on this PT Cruiser. But it sure looks cool.

Some Real Fire Effects

9 A cartoon bulldog combined with blazing real fire behind a peeled-back surface. It looks right at home on this tuner car.

10 A flaming skeleton riding a bike is very appropriate for the back of this motorcycle trailer. Artwork by Mike Ellwood.

11 Very neat idea here. It's a dragon graphic shadowed against a fire on the hood.

Gathering Ideas

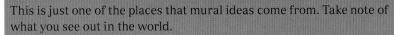

This is just one of the places that mural ideas come from. Take note of what you see out in the world.

12 Flaming machine gun gangster skeleton on the hood of a Ford Ranger.

13 Elvis as a skeleton devil living large in Hell's Vegas?

14 This is a very clever mural. An eagle flying and the wings turning into flames, yet the bottom flames are actually feathers.

Nature Murals

15 This car is basecoated with a very soft pearl, so it makes sense that the mural is airbrushed in a soft, graceful style. The eagle position fits the hood quite effectively.

16 Stylized eagle mural I did on a Corvette.

17 What is interesting about this mural is where it was done, inside a panel on the side of the car. This kind of layout would work very well with a stock paint job. Note that the tail fin is behind the panel, yet the front fin hangs over the edge, adding depth.

18 Here, Ron Gibbs has airbrushed a wolf mural on the entire side of a pickup truck.

19 Here's the other side of the truck, but this time there's a deer. Note how both murals feature a stream down the middle of the door, creating an optical illusion of greater width.

20 Ron painted this garden-themed bug a few years ago. The design layout and artwork are extraordinary. Observe all the detail.

21 Look at how Ron did the hood. Again with something long, in this case a road, running down it. This gives the illusion of great depth.

22 Close-up of the artwork. The detail and sense of perspective are unreal.

23 Close up of Ron's undersea artwork.

24 Another of Ron's amazing tailgate murals. This time it's undersea and goes perfectly with the dark blue basecoat.

Other Murals

25 Put this under the category of "don't know what it is, but it sure looks cool." The green tones are very powerful.

26 A story and a mural on the bed of this truck.

27 Close-up of the artwork. Look closely; it is very detailed and beautifully done. Art by Kent Ford, Auto Art Studio.

28 Detail shot from a different beach mural by Ron Gibbs. Look closely at the way the various textures were painted. The surface of the water, the hair, the edges of the waves.

29 Mickey Harris is famous for his amazing mural work. This is the Heroes truck he painted, dedicated to the events and heroes of 9/11. Note the color scheme, the soft tones that were used. It keeps this mural from being overbearing.

30 Very cool beach scene complete with classic cars and a truck. Artwork by Ron Gibbs. Note how it differs from the first picture in this chapter.

31 Can you tell this mural was done by the same person? Mickey's soft tones are very distinctive. Look at the way the dark meets up with the light, featuring the only hot colors in the mural.

32 How about a woman's face on a hood? This artwork was most likely done over the silver basecoat using black and white tones. Then candy red was applied.

33 The Joker mural by Cory Saint Clair. Quite a contrast from the previous murals. Simple, just a face, black and white tones with a bit of red, yet extremely powerful.

34 Very interesting technique used for the Joker's hair. The hair turns into smoke.

35 This pin-up witch that I painted fits nicely on this Nissan truck hood.

36 The hood of Michael Ludwig's '96 Dodge truck features a mural of his wife's face.

37 The tailgate of the truck. Michael's truck was painted by Patrick Kelly and is an amazing work of art. Note the surreal blue fire and how the blue is used as a light source.

38 The artwork on this truck features a bio-mechanical theme but uses the blue fire to frame it. Look at how the artwork is laid out on the side of the truck.

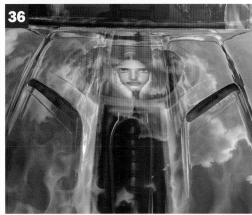

39 There are so many things going on in this mural. Each of the skulls is different. And this side of the truck is different from the other side.

40 Close-up of the mural. Check out the way the artist lit the mural. The blue tones are reflected by the fire on the skulls and structure in the mural.

41 This extreme close-up shows the degree of depth that can be achieved with careful airbrushing. Note the wetness of the eye, the hard bone effect of the skull, and the cold aged steel.

42 And the door jambs were not forgotten, as the artwork wraps around into them.

43 A close-up reveals that there are all kinds of skeletons and creatures lurking. Note the use of similar colors.

44 Wild artwork. But is it a mural or graphic?

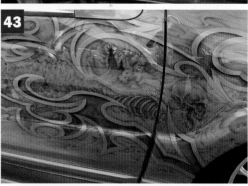

45 Ron Gibbs did an amazing paint job on this Ford truck. A dark, almost black, to light blue face was done, and then tribal artwork was applied.

46 Detail from the tailgate of the truck. The artwork was done under the candy blue.

47 Don't overlook good ideas just because you don't agree with all the artwork. There are a few good ideas on this truck. But let's say you don't like lightning—well, don't miss the other good ideas, such as the way the graphic frames the artwork.

Advertising with Graphics

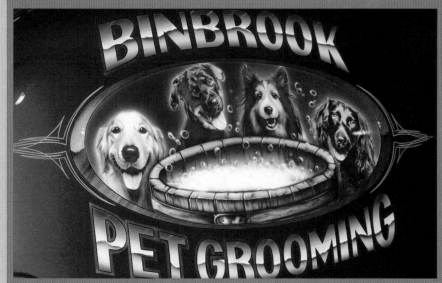

Mural work is not just for show cars—it is also a great way to promote your business. Here, on this PT Cruiser, Ron Gibbs painted a mural to promote the owner's dog grooming business.

For this dog training business, the owner had his painter create a mural of a German shepherd with trick lettering.

1

Old Paint?

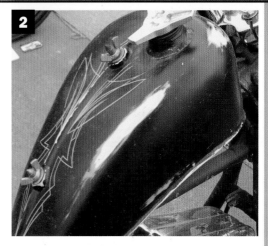

2

The newest trend in custom paint is actually old paint, or paint that is applied using various techniques in order to look old. The popularity of this paint is growing as it is complete opposite of new, shiny paint. Sometimes the old paint is untouched and actually quite old with rust that shows through, as seen on Michael Jacobs's 1929 Model A. Or an old finish that artwork has been applied to as seen on Bill Steele's drag car. Or it can it can be painted to look old, as seen on Richard Begg's 1931 Ford. But no matter what the process, the appeal of this style of finish is based on history. It shows the patina of the passing years. All the experiences and history the vehicle has been through. The story of the vehicle as seen on the surface. Old paint lends itself to "imagination" to "dream and conceive." Old paint tells a story as to where or what the car might of gone through in its history. A newly finished and fresh car that's been done

to perfection is wonderful and fun to look at, but how often do you look at one and wonder what it would be like to drive it, or what the owner is like? Or where did all those wild and interesting parts come from? The new cars have their place and show real craftmanship. The old cars, all rusty and wildly put together, do just the same. And most of the roughly finished cars are truly driven and enjoyed. The owners take pride in the use of their hot rods. Both are right and both have their place. Old looking paint jobs or old cars with original paint have a warmth of character, set a unique trend, and can go places that most finished cars just can't. No two old rusty rat rods will ever look the same. Unique is choice in the world of hot rods and customs.

1 Hot rods with old, worn, and rusty paint are called rat rods, like Bill Steele's old drag car. The reddish basecoat is the actual old finish, but the artwork was applied and then lightly sanded with a sanding pad to appear worn.

2 Extremely cool "worn out" paint. Did you notice the blue midcoat and how it plays so effectively against the white and flat finish topcoat?

3 Believe it or not, the "rusty" finish on this '31 Ford was actually painted on. The owner, Richard Beggs, devoted countless hours to perfecting this rust finish.

4 The back half of Richard's '31 Ford. Note the skull head on the gas door.

5 Stripe over rust? Why not?

6 Check out the color scheme on the hood of this Chevy. The yellow and white striping brings out the rich earth tones of the rusty surface.

7 This Harley-Davidson Knucklehead features paint colors that appear to be faded, which goes great with the worn-out look.

8 I don't know the story on this paint, but it sure looks genuinely old. Most likely the artwork was added recently on this 1950s Chevy ¾-ton truck.

9 Old paint on the surface, air bag suspension, and high-tech drivetrain inside this 1940 Ford Tudor.

10 Was chalk used here for these roughly shaped flames on this 1931 Ford coupe? It looks as though the flames were merely rat rod graffiti. Looks cool and very different.

11 Nash Motorcycle Co. does some cutting-edge retro custom paint on their bikes. Notice the old-style layout of the lettering, how it is shaped.

12 "Cooter's Marriage Counseling and Auto Repair." Bill Steele's 1958 Chevy, painted to look old.

13 The real thing or retro paint on this Chevy truck? Sure looks real.

14 Here's the real thing: old paint with actual rust. The paint on Mike Jacobs's 1929 Model A is from the 1950s and has worn away over time.

15 Very brutal 1928 Ford rag top. Very clean, and the whitewalls are perfect on it.

16 The designer on this wild little Ford truck was thinking outside the box. Very unique.

17 Adam Parnell's '72 VW Bug is about as low budget as paint gets. Spray bomb primer gray and random graphics.

18 No rust here, just a no-nonsense, old-style drag car paint job on a 1937 Ford that looks brand-new.

19 Beautifully executed striping and a satin finish black say it all on this 1935 Ford.

20 Small details working together to create a big impact on this 1949 Ford Crown Vic hot rod.

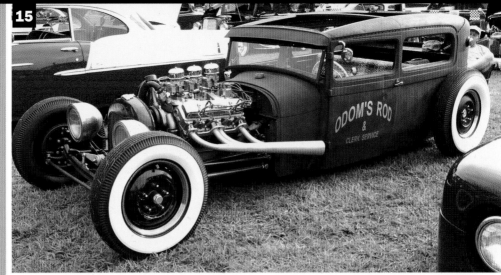

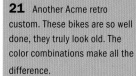

21 Another Acme retro custom. These bikes are so well done, they truly look old. The color combinations make all the difference.

22 Retro done without looking worn on this early 1930s Ford truck. Very subtle yet sharp paint on this truck.

23 No rust here, just bare metal and brutal retro artwork. Pure evil 1931 Ford.

24 Ron Anderson's '50 rockabilly Chevy pickup stands out with its ground metal fenders.

25 Yes, that is real rust covering the surface of Ben Jordan's 1935 Chevy truck. And he has no plans to ever paint it.

26 The top of the previous tank. Old-style striping that was most likely partially removed with a sanding pad.

27 Obviously retro paint, but it is well done and the artwork is very clever. Note the cracked black of the panel.

28 The artwork on this Sucker Punch Sally bike is pure retro. Done with a brush. Check out the sanded away "worn" basecoat. Note the use of lime green. It just sets off the whole paint job.

Is Flat Black Out of Style?

Some people say flat black has been done too much. But the unique and clean body style of this early 1950s Chevy sedan seems perfect for a plain, flat black finish.

For complete design harmony to go with the copper lines, orange rims, a one-off headlamp, and other trick features, flat black is the only choice for this HD Knucklehead.

Here, pinstriped flames work very effectively on this satin-finish sedan.

1

The Very
Best

Most people are used to seeing masterpieces hanging on the wall of museums. But many legendary works of art roll out on the road, art that was created by master fine artists, art that can withstand rain, wind, and dirt, and will always be timeless. This chapter is a tribute to those incredible artists.

2

1 The best airbrushing I've ever done was this Stevie Ray Vaughan tank. Bike by Monty King.

2 Bustin' out. Bill makes it look easy to achieve the kind of perspective that makes a mural like this work so effectively.

3 The top of the skull flame bike. Note the reflective glow of the skull's eyes. Now count the skulls.

4 Bill's infamous skull flame paint. The layers and depth are unreal.

5 An underlayer of artwork with Bill's very distinctive lightning over it. The softness of his airbrushing in unequalled.

Bill Streeter

Bill Streeter is an airbrush artist from East Haven, Connecticut. Bill grew up in a very artistic household. His dad was an artist, and Bill started airbrushing on bikes while in his teens for a bike shop in Florida called C & L Hog. His work began to appear in magazines such as *Easyriders* in the 1970s, and Bill influenced a whole generation of airbrush artists. It would not be a stretch to say that Bill is the godfather of modern-day custom bike airbrushing. Most every airbrush artist out there today grew up seeing those images of Bill's artwork in the magazines.

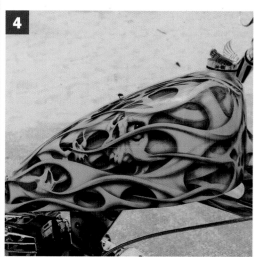

6

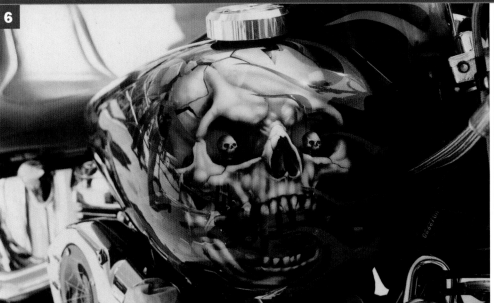

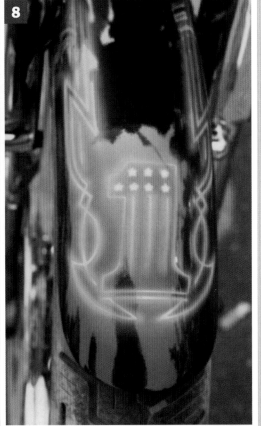

6 His legendary break-apart skull paint job. So real.

7 No one airbrushes neon effect quite so well. Look closely at the eagle and how it is lit.

8 Simple and beautiful.

9 One of Bill's famous tanks for C & L Hog. There are so many things going on in this mural. The use of darks and lights is incredible.

10 A layer of fire and a layer of cracked metal–effect graphics.

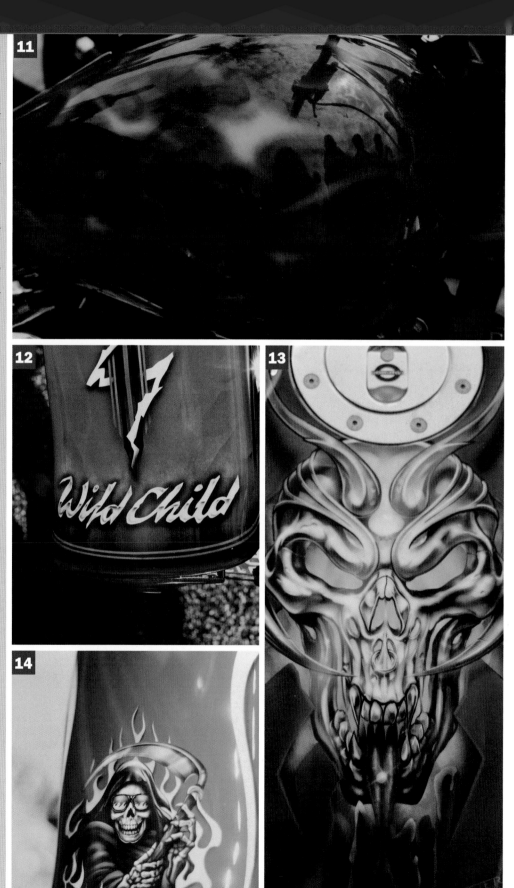

11 My personal favorite Streeter paint job: endless layers of flames and nearly abstract.

12 Even his lettering has that soft, surreal effect.

13 Is this skull made of metal or bone? Bill paints it to look like both.

14 Another well-known paint job is his "Too Bad" mural. Look closely at the detail and the color design.

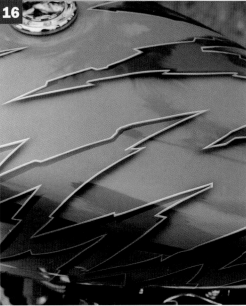

15 One of Bill's best-known paint jobs is his wizard holding the world. Try to count all the various things happening in this mural.

16 Even simple graphics have more punch when Bill paints them. The depth here makes these graphics stand out.

17 Look closely at these flames, the colors, the movement, and the way they bring out the best aspects of the bike.

18 The legendary Ghetto Blaster chop from C & L Hog.

19 "Drug Crazed Thugs." Check out the portrait of James Dean on the front of this tank.

20 Notice the way this mural was put together, with the eyes and the lightning hitting the ground and releasing a skeleton.

21 Only Bill could come up with a welder cutting his way out of a gas tank.

22 One of the most amazing murals ever done. Check out the steel snakes, the beveled edged flames, and the unreal soft, surreal face.

23

24

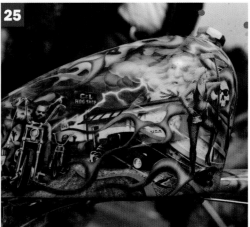

25

26

27

28

23 Another C & L Hog mural filled with wild details. Too many to even list here.

24 Bill painted this Camel Roadhouse bike for Eddie Trotta. The graphic idea here is so unique and original.

25 The C & L Hog Tattoo bike. Too many details to count.

26 Rear fender of the Tattoo bike. Look closely.

27 Bill's flames are unreal. So original.

28 His flames have such dimension and depth.

29 Even more depth with endless layers.

30 Bill painted this street rod back in the 1990s.

31 But on the trunk of the car is a mural of the car.

32 Another Streeter car mural, this time on a bike. The creativity is endless.

Simple Beauty

Great artwork does not always have to be wild and extravagant. This simple graphic is amazing in its simple, colorful beauty.

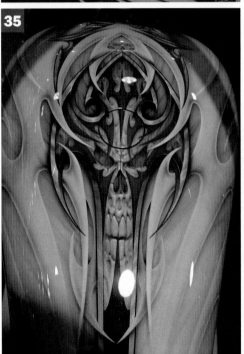

33 My favorite Streeter mural, the Harley-Davidson tank with a spirit eagle flying above.

34 One last Streeter mural, showing the movement his work is famous for.

Mike Terwilliger

35 Mike Terwilliger is an airbrush artist from Long Island, New York, and creates some of the most finely detailed airbrush artwork there is.

Fitto

36 Fitto is an airbrush artist out of Canada who does some evil twist work.

37 His use of limited colors gives his work a unique look.

43

44

45

Keith Hanson

Keith Hanson works with Dave Perewitz to create some of the most sleek and harmonious motorcycle art on the planet.

43 Keith's use of color and airbrush technique is too perfect, putting together red, green, and gold.

44 One of my favorite paint jobs, Joe Pro's custom Perewitz bike.

45 He has a great sense of sleek simplicity, making the best use of the space provided for his art.

Dawne Holmes

There is no finer technical airbrush artist than Dawne Holmes of Prescott, Arizona.

46 She is unequaled, from this cartoon breaking the glass of a bike tank panel...

47 to a simple ribbon floating on a fender...

48 to endless layers of graphics on an oil tank.

49 Examine the way she put this mural together. The way the artwork goes onto the neck of the bike.

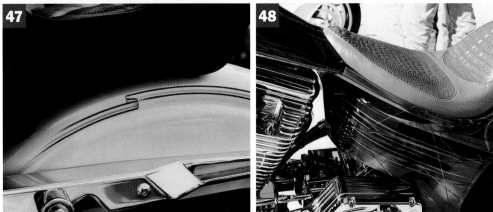

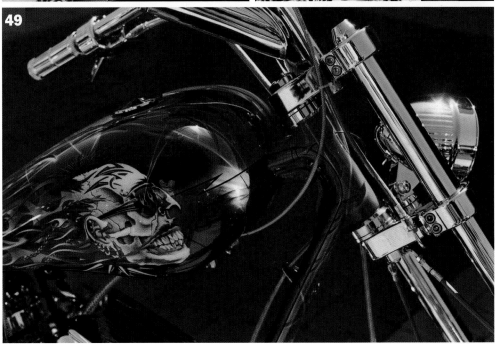

50 The way these colors all work together creates such an impact...

51 from total simplicity like this incredible stylized eagle...

52 to an airplane as an eagle with a vortex behind it. Only Dawne can do this.

53 Her best-known creation is the Harley-Davidson Biker Blues bike.

54 All you see was airbrushed on. That is not a decal, it is paint. It took her over 300 hours to paint this bike.

And a Few Last Treats
55 I don't know the artist, but this design is so effective for this bike. It is an example of less being more.

56 I saw this bike at Sturgis in 2006 and the artwork is out of this world. Note the depth and dimension.

57 The oil tank on Carla Doll's Redneck Mutant. No human skulls. She digs fish, so the artist painted fish skeletons.

58 Some of the most amazing artwork is found on lowriders. Here, a combination of graphics, silver leaf, and airbrush artwork combine to create a rolling masterpiece.

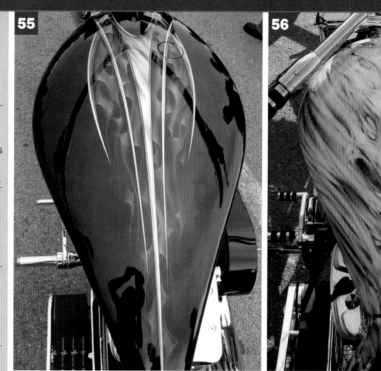

Index

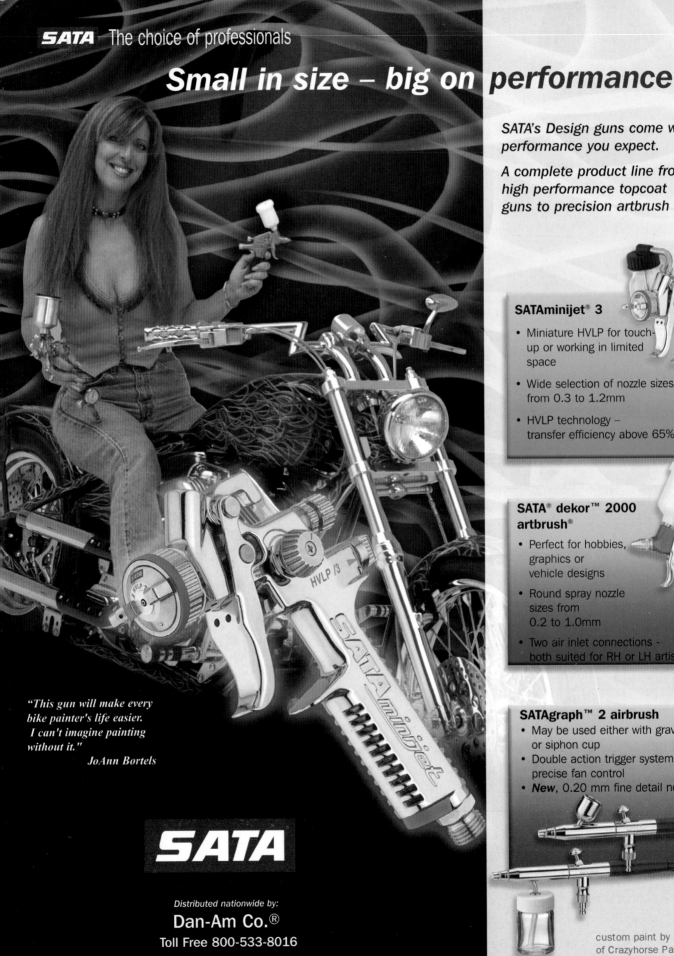
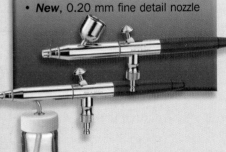